PANDEMIC,

PENGUIN POOP,

&

POND SCUM

MARK HURST

Pandemic, Penguin Poop, & Pond Scum

Mark Hurst

Copyright 2021 Mark Hurst

All rights reserved.

Cover & Interior Design: Mark Hurst and Greg Jarrard

Production: K Christoffersen of BookWise Publishing

Publisher: Preservation Books

Library of Congress Control Number: Pending

ISBN: 978-1-60645-343-8

10/10/2023 version

TABLE OF CONTENTS

PANDEMIC,
PENGUIN POOP,
&
POND SCUM

INTRODUCTION

The Covid pandemic has been a massive disruption to our way of life. The quarantine and isolation have messed with our emotions, causing us to look at the world through a cloudy, lonely lens where we see mostly gray, murky futures. Even those of us who are eternal optimists wonder if it will ever go away. We long for normalcy. The Beatles sang, "It's been a long, cold, lonely winter. It feels like years since it's been here."

This is how we feel. Less and less hopefulness. Increasing helplessness. When will it end?

This book doesn't have many answers about the end of the dreariness and very few suggestions for getting through the muck. It's just a collection of observations about everyday goings-on, life chugging forward through the Covid maze. It's a little bit of personal introspection, a touch of humor, a touch of curiousness. Nothing revelatory, more mundane than magical. Peculiarities, not a prescription.

I hope it might be something of a pandemic pick-me-up, a mashup of musings about finding joy in everything we do. Even on the cloudiest of days. I've shared with you these, wildly, disparate observations, gleaned on the road to normalcy. I hope this cheers you up a bit. I've gained a bit of strength writing instead of sitting around pouting about the giant Covid cloud that came along and ruined our normally peaceful picnic.

PENGUIN POOP

ere is, perhaps, the most interesting headline ever written. It's not about terrorism, or civilians flying in space, or Biden falling asleep in his soup. It's not about earthquakes or hurricanes, or cataclysmic events.

Here it is:

Antarctic Penguin Poop Emits Laughing Gas

I dare you to find a more compelling news story. CNN reported the findings of some scientists in Antarctica who spend their careers mucking about in Penguin guano. (I'm tempted to say CNN does much of the same thing, but let's move on.)

Here's the interesting thing I discovered in an article posted on EcoWatch, a blog/watchdog group, written by Jordan Davidson.

"After nosing about in guano for several hours, one goes completely cuckoo," lead researcher Bo Elberling said; "One begins to feel ill and get a headache.

"Penguin poop is known to create huge amounts of nitrous oxide because the penguins' diet is rich in fish and krill that have absorbed large amounts of nitrogen via phytoplankton. The nitrogen is then released from the guano. When it hits the soil and interacts with the air, it is converted to nitrous oxide.

"Nitrous oxide is a potent greenhouse gas, with a

1

warming effect that is 300 times what carbon dioxide produces, according to Newsweek. It's also used as a sedative for dental procedures, as a recreational drug and in agriculture."

It's that very last line, "also used as a sedative for dental procedures" that caught my attention.

If you've ever used laughing gas at the dentist's office, you know that it's fantastic. There are no hallucinatory effects; you don't get high on nitrous oxide. It's not a mind-altering drug. You don't get addicted. But going in for a root canal is a different experience. You feel relaxed, comfortable, and feel like telling the dentist to "Drill away. Bring it on, Doc. Take your best shot."

Now, I'm not advocating that we legalize nitrous oxide like they've done in Denmark. The Danish people use it all the time, recreationally. But it might be helpful if you're terrified of speaking in front of a bunch of people, for instance. Perhaps you have a performance review with your boss, and you're freaking out with worry. Maybe it's the first time you meet your new in-laws. Maybe the first time you meet your future wife. Or taking the LSAT or other tests of your intelligence. Imagine what a little bit of nitrous could do for your anxiety in these difficult moments.

Would it be so wrong to have a little snort of laughing gas every now and then? Just for painful, root-canalish types of moments. We've legalized medical marijuana, and we're getting comfortable with that decision. So far, the country hasn't gone to hell as predicted.

Nitrous oxide is unlikely to ruin the country. After all, it's laughing gas. It is meant to calm and soothe anxiety. There's never been a time in history where a dose of laughter has been needed more. We are all cranky. We are all a little angry, frustrated, polarized. The news is always grim. I say bring in some penguins. They'd certainly be welcome to stay in my orchard or the corral.

There are any number of occasions where a little nitrous oxide would be a welcome relief. Here's an example. At your Thanksgiving table this year, there is likely to be someone who starts flinging stuffing at in-laws who think the oppressive government wants us to do something painfully easy, like wearing a mask. Before there is an all-out internecine war, please pass the nitrous oxide. What a happy Thanksgiving we'll have this year!

There's doom and gloom all around us in the days of a pandemic. Polemic politics plague us. But pay attention to the news coming out of Antarctica. Yes, too much nitrous oxide may be bad for the environment, but don't dwell on this. For goodness sake, it's laughing gas! Free laughing gas for all. Not a bad thing.

Here is my takeaway: You can find good, even in a pile of poop.

I AM POND SCUM.

WELL, ACTUALLY LOWER.

I'M LIKE THE FUNGUS

THAT FEEDS ON POND SCUM.

JULIA ROBERTS IN MY BEST FRIEND'S WEDDING

POND SCUM

During my career in marketing, I was introduced to some extremely bright people at Utah State University, in Logan, Utah. I have met any number of researchers and engineers working on projects to help farmers with a few things related to water, growing and raising crops, and being good citizens of the planet.

I met an interesting young man, a farm boy. A very bright farm boy. Without all the scientific sizzle, here is a very brief description of a clever idea he came up with. This is my version, and it's close enough to tell the story and make a point.

This farm boy was regularly tasked with feeding the cows, mowing the hay, tilling the fields, irrigating the fields, working sunup to sundown; his calloused hands the evidence of a tough life on the farm. One other unpleasant task. He routinely had to pull algae off the top of irrigation holding ponds so the water could keep flowing to the crops.

Algae. Pond scum. It grows on standing fresh water and is a bane, as bad or worse than weeds in the garden. You must clean it off from time to time. Our farm boy hated this chore.

It's nasty-looking stuff. Some people wonder if algae is a plant, lacking leaves, stem, and root. But it does survive with a form of photosynthesis, converting sunlight, CO2 and a few nutrients, including nitrogen and phosphorous, into material known as biomass. The most complex freshwater forms of algae are the charophyta, or green algae which includes, for example, spirogyra and stoneworts. (Spyro gyra was also a funky band in the 1970s. Hard to tell if they knew this meant pond scum, but never mind about that.)

As he grew up, this young man was always curious about algae and began to turn that curiosity into science. It turns out algae isn't a bad thing. It may be a very good thing. He learned that algae could be grown, cultivated, dried and aged, and turned into diesel fuel. Pond scum, the lowliest of noxious, nefarious, agricultural nemeses, might possibly become a cash crop.

Our farm boy, a budding scientist, would clean up his ponds, and ponder. He would spend days considering ways to pull the green globs of goo off the water and somehow save them for experimentation. The answer wasn't in textbooks up on campus. The answer was one-hundred yards away.

A sprinkler. All over the fields were large motor-driven wheels that automate irrigation, moving pipe around large areas, reducing manual labor.

He hypothesized that if he could use the wheels, the motors, and some ingenuity, he could drag cotton rope through the algae, collect the plants, dry them in the sun like so many shirts on a clothesline, then harvest them for experimentation. His theory became reality.

He has a long way to go but his contraption worked, and it's being implemented as part of his PhD in agriculture. He is turning pond scum into a renewable energy source to reduce our dependence on fossil fuels. A farm boy. A brilliant young man who looked at the slimy, stinky stuff and saw possibilities. In the muck he saw opportunity.

He used existing hardware, some rope from Walmart, and set about changing a farmer's bane into an economic boon.

I admired his thoughtful insights and his patient approach as he lived and worked the land. Where others saw waste, he saw wonder. He didn't see dreck, he saw dreams. He didn't see scum; he saw a scientific opportunity. He no longer saw the mess; he saw a miracle.

For the last eighteen months, Covid algae formed on our fresh-water lives. Our blessed lives of rich abundance came, nearly, to a frightening halt. All around us we saw unemployment soar, small businesses closed their doors, children stayed home from school. Nightly news brought us pictures of vacant American cities with streets hauntingly empty of human life. Everyone on the planet had a taste of prison life; locked up, isolated, frightened.

We also witnessed innovation. We saw resiliency. We saw American strength and ingenuity go to work to get the pond scum off the water. Restaurants kept cooking food and delivery services brought it to our door or our car. Hollywood released movies on streaming services so we could stay entertained. School administrators accelerated home-based learning. Collaborative technology like Zoom kept people working from home, and the predicted economic crash didn't happen. We saw creative people do amazing things. It was a nation with sleeves rolled up.

Despite our very best efforts to avoid the virus, I got it. It was very mild, and my gratitude quotient soared. Many of us felt helpless as millions of people suffered excruciating deaths while healthcare workers, exhausted physically and emotionally drained, stayed and stood their post.

Regulators got out of the way, and a vaccine was developed in record time. We saw what was possible under pressure. Our best moments came from desperation.

At the very beginning of the pandemic, we felt like we had been cursed. It wasn't too much of an exaggeration to believe it was the end of days. Covid was, indeed, a curse. In the black of night, in the dark of alleyways, it crept in on quiet kitty-feet, the silent predator, then pounced. It was a killer, mutating and daily changing its disguise. It was extremely aggressive and isn't going away anytime soon.

But we feel like we are winning. I joined premature celebrants and took off my mask, declared victory far too soon and then, in a sobering set-back, a friend of fifty years suddenly died from Covid complications. There's no victory just yet. I kept my mask on for quite a while. (And might be putting in back on regularly soon.)

But we're not afraid anymore; we're not paralyzed. We're moving again, getting out of jail. If we are a bit to zealous, a bit too careless, it's because we are tough. We are strong and face challenges courageously. We have had enough. Toughness may sound, to some, like arrogance or ignorant denial. I think it is nothing of the kind. I think it is a farm kid going to Walmart for some cotton rope, finding new ways to solve a problem and with that rope and a few spare parts we are pulling ourselves out of the scum and finding new ways to celebrate life and the extraordinary strength of the human spirit.

I don't believe curses come from God. They are just part of the deal. In whatever form curses come, regardless of the misery that follows, we do find purpose, and strength is always at the other end. Always. You may be like me, hesitant to call Covid a blessing. It's path of destruction is a little too fresh. But it will be a blessing, or one of its many variants. There will be a day when, with masks finally off for good, we will all breathe more deeply, love one another more fervently, and hold on tighter to things that matter most.

Bring on the curses, we'll beat them. Bring on the scum. We'll find something to do with it.

MERIT BADGES

ARE "EARNED"

BY MANY MOTHERS . . .

AND FATHERS . . .

AND BY SOME BOY SCOUTS.

AUTHOR ANONYMOUS

MERIT BADGE COUNSELOR

I am a wood carver. This is a hobby I picked up some thirty years ago, quite by chance.

When I was a young man, family vacations were spent camping in the mountains and forests of Idaho, Wyoming, Montana. Evening entertainment was sitting around the campfire, singing, snacking, playing games. During the day we fished and hiked. And when nothing else was going on I would pick up a stick and whittle away on it. Not carving anything, just whittling. I learned how to sharpen a knife, keep it sharp, and make a pile of shavings, wood chips, useless pieces of pine the victim of my razor-sharp blade.

Many years later, my wife challenged me to make something from a wooden stick, other than a mess. I took up the challenge and began, what would become, a hobby that produced hundreds of animal heads, walking sticks, and folk-art interpretations of Santa Claus. It's a very messy hobby, thousands of wood chips flying through the air, in vain, trying to catch them all on my enormous canvas drop cloth.

I've never turned carving into anything other than a curious pastime. I've been asked many times to sell some of my finished pieces. I don't. People urge me to replicate them, put them up for sale on the Internet and turn it into a business. Not interested.

Once a year all the Santas come out of storage and fill our home with their stiff, woody ways, a delight to kids, friends and neighbors who like to come by and see how many new ones I've made. The one-night-only parade now includes hot chocolate, cinnamon rolls and lots of children who love to touch them, something I encourage, contrary to overly cautious mothers terrified of breakage. "They are made from a fairly hard wood, and they won't break," I tell them. Many of the Santas now have gooey, cinammony, chocolaty fingerprints on them, a permanent reminder of the delight these wooden figurines bring to the sticky faces and wondrous eyes of the children who visit the display.

A couple of women, on separate occasions, came by and admired my art. One of them was responsible for art exhibitions and contests at the junior high school in our neighborhood. She thought I was artistic and asked me to judge the entries one year and I was glad to do it even though I still don't consider myself an artist. Eventually I did this, not only for her school, but I became a regular at the high school show, elementary schools, and other community events where I would award ribbons to young artists for their painting, drawing, photography, sculpting, and mixed media which may include videos and digital art.

The second woman was involved with scouting and by involved, I mean she was a driving force in getting her five boys through the program, each with their Eagle Scout. When they couldn't find anyone in the area to teach wood carving, I agreed to become a merit badge counselor. I read through the materials and began teaching the fundamentals and helping the boys complete a carving.

On one occasion, this same mother, a chilling doppelgänger of Captain Queeg, called to schedule a class for one of her sons and his friend. A class of two is just about right, although a single student is better. This involves handling a very sharp knife and one-on-

one oversight is important. I agreed to take two scouts together. Word got out that I was doing a class, and on the afternoon of the scheduled event, twelve boys showed up. I glared at Captain Queeg, a non-verbal stare down meant to say, "What are you trying to do?" She is tough, the mother of eight or nine kids and her pursed lips and icy stare back at me said, "Figure it out. Right now."

There are four separate tasks the boys must learn in order to earn their merit badge. First, safety. Second, first aid for those who didn't listen to the safety training. Third, sharpening, the reason you teach first aid. And, finally, the techniques of carving.

"Show me your knives," I said as I began the class. "Did you each bring a knife?" They were told in advance they needed a parent to make sure they had a knife. They all followed instructions, each arriving with a knife ranging from a hunting knife like the one used in the Jeff Bridges movie, "Jagged Edge," to a tiny one-blade key fob with "Dave's Body Shop" engraved on the side. The hunting knife was going to remove fingers and possibly an entire hand if I allowed the kid to use it. The key fob blade wouldn't cut paper. The sharpness factor of the other blades ranged somewhere between dull, duller, and dullest. Most kitchen butter knives had a sharper edge than the odd assortment of tools that showed up. Cardboard has a sharper edge. Toast would be a possible replacement.

Our goal was to have each boy make a small, simple neckerchief slide based on the "Minions" from the animated movie. "Let's begin," I reluctantly blurted out. I gave each boy a small block of wood that that I had cut from my personal supply, which would become their own Minion when finished.

"We will cover four areas today. Safety, first aid, sharpening, and techniques. Do not, I repeat, do not pick up your knife and start carving until we get through the requirements." They were fondling their wood blocks, tossing them in the air, smelling the woody fragrance, anything but listening to me.

"Let's start with safety. Here are the things you need to . . ."

"Ahhhhhhhhhhh." One minute and twelve seconds into the class and we already had our first "Ahhhhhhhhhhh." I hadn't written a single word about safety on my erasable white board before one of our Eagle Scout candidates put dull blade to wood, slipped and cut his finger. The only reason he didn't sever the digit was because his blade was so dull. It did, however, make a nasty gash. Blood started dripping everywhere including the tile floor of my basement family-room/art studio.

The kid looked at the blood, turned a whiter shade of pale, and dropped to the ground. Fainted. The woman who arranged the class, Captain Queeg, looked at the blood and fainted. My wife was in the room and took charge, not because she was a nurse but because her tile floor was awash in blood. (Awash may be the exaggeration of the fiction writer in me, but it was a significant wound.)

The other eleven boys went silent, most of them slightly queasy, each of them unsure if they needed the wood carving merit badge of if they could try drawing, or painting, or raising pigeons instead. When I was their age, I enjoyed the merit badge on animal husbandry.

I was the only one who carved a Minion neckerchief slide that day. I told the boys that none of the knives were acceptable. They would never be sharp enough to carve wood. I explained the twisted logic that the sharper the blade, the safer the knife.

Their pale faces looked confused. I told them, "If your blade is dull you will have to push harder and harder to remove even a single chip of wood. A dull knife will slip off the wood instead of cutting the wood. Each one of you is going to cut a finger. Guaranteed."

I had their attention.

We walked them through safety precautions, then through a few first aid tips. The three mothers in the room were giving a live demonstration of first aid on our bloody patient. Final requirement, other than carving, demonstrate how to sharpen a blade, grinding, polishing, stropping.

I then carved a Minion neckerchief slide. It was imperfect but it was quick, and it was done. I even painted it with the blue overalls and yellow head of the cartoon character and ended the class. "You all have to go home and have your father help with the carving. You are welcome to borrow some of my sharp tools, but you must have the supervision and oversight of at least one parent and a paramedic standing by.

I don't think the kid with the cut finger ever finished his project. But eight of the twelve scouts did. A few fathers took me up on the offer to use my professional-grade tools and helped their sons fashion a finished project.

I continued to judge art shows for a time but discontinued my woodcarving merit badge counseling. Risky business. Maybe I was a coward. Maybe it was the risk of blood on the flood and the threat of lawsuits, reckless endangerment of kids. Instead, I became a counselor for public speaking and citizenship in the community merit badges. (A very different form of knives come out in government forums.)

I continue to think about those dull knives. Too dull to carve a simple piece of wood, just dangerous enough to slice a finger. I thought about how the boys wanted to forego safety training and start carving immediately. They didn't want to be bothered with first-aid training even though I emphasized how frequently I cut myself. When you use sharp tools, you are going to get cut from time to time. I showed them all my scars.

They had no interest in hearing even a single mention of the fundamental creed of the Boy Scouts, "Be Prepared." They didn't want to prepare; they didn't care about the dangers. They believed, unwisely, that nothing bad would happen to them, drawn, like all boys, to the glimmering allure of a sharp knife.

The boy scouts learned a lot about sharp knives that day. The parents of the boys, and all parents everywhere, learn that they are all artists, attempting, to shape children into pieces of art, chip by chip, a sharp knife making occasional deep cuts along the way. There is no training. There is no discussion of preparation, or safety awareness. We simply pick up the raw wood and begin carving, whittling away. We struggle, we make mistakes, our hands are tired. And some of us, on occasion, feel compelled to return home and ask our Dads' for help, realizing how unprepared we are to raise a child, how feeble our attempts are to fashion a piece of artwork that someone may adjudge to be a "blue ribbon," fearing that our attempts have left our carving a little too rough around the edges. Still, we whittle away, still we struggle, a sharp edge in hand, methodically shaping young men and women, our rough-hewn chunks of wood, into award-winning works of art, made beautiful by the loving care, time and patience, nicks, cuts, and bandages of amateur woodcarvers, who will earn neither a badge nor a trophy, but painstakingly, lovingly toil away, shaping the finished piece. And by any measure it is a masterpiece.

CHOOSY MOTHERS

CHOOSE

JIF . . .

.M. Smucker Company

ARTIFICIAL INGREDIENTS

As a kid growing up, we could choose between Cheerios and Corn Flakes for breakfast. Or oatmeal. That was it. Two choices. Reportedly, there were other choices, but we didn't have them in our cupboard. We didn't know other options were available.

It's a different story today. There are dozens of choices in the very crowded cereal aisle. When grandchildren come for a visit, the first think I do is head to the grocery store and stock up on sugary cereals denied them by their fussy mothers. I don't think kids will die from eating tasty cereal instead of wallpaper paste. I hide the boxes from their mothers, but they have caught on to my ruse. They don't like it, but they tolerate it.

My oldest grandson, now a married adult, remembers being spoiled at my house when he was growing up, and now shares my passion for great cereal. Just recently, he dropped by with a jumbo-sized bag of Cocoa Puffs, one of my favorites.

This wasn't just an ordinary bag of Cocoa Puffs. This was a limited-edition version, something rare and very special. The manufacturers added Lucky Charm marshmallows. You know, the stars and moons of the leprechaun's cereal. They're not just good, they are "magically delicious." And combining the colorful marshmallow nuggets with chocolate puffs is a completely new level of gourmet morning entrees. Thanks to my favorite grandchild, Cole Eades, for this discovery. (Attention all grandchildren, everywhere. This is the type of thing grandparents are looking for as we make our annual selection of 'Favorite'. We adore all the hand-drawn pictures you send, the letters you write, the back-to-school photos. These things matter. But what we really want is bribery. Goodies, cookies, candy, you decide. Cole has raised the bar and set a new standard in payola.)

The bag of Cocoa Puffs revealed one other thing I hadn't seen before. Right there on the front of the bag, in very large letters was this: "Made with real Cocoa." I know there are some unhealthy ingredients in breakfast cereals, preservatives, flavorings, and, of course, a couple of scoops of sugar. But this was new to me. "Real Cocoa?" Is it necessary to tell me they use 'real cocoa? If you don't use real chocolate in a chocolate cereal, what do you use? Brown sawdust?

Suddenly, this "real" notification started showing up on all sorts of things. Cheese-it crackers are made with real cheese. Kraft macaroni uses powdered cheese the color of a Halloween pumpkin but insists it is real cheese. I've never seen cheese that shade of neon orange.

Real honey. I saw a documentary about the declining population of bees and the ensuing criminal activity of manufacturing and distributing fake honey, made of mostly corn syrup.

Ever check your pancake syrup? There's a reason why they call it pancake syrup. It's because it doesn't have a drop of real maple syrup in it, just flavoring. Try real Vermont maple syrup some time and you'll taste the difference. Caution, you'll never want to go back to other 'fake' brands.

I started using Almond Milk a few years ago as an alternative to dairy. Farmers don't like it. They claim

Almond milk isn't milk. I saw a t-shirt with this on it: "Real milk comes from tits. Almonds don't have tits."

Here's a curious one: Mayonnaise is now made with real ingredients. I can't imagine what a bottle of fake mayonnaise may have included. It has always been a mysterious food, but now, at the very least, it is real.

My bottle of mustard claims it's now 100% natural. I didn't know there was fake mustard.

I grabbed a quick breakfast one morning, a "Kellogg's Nutrigrain soft baked breakfast bar made with real fruit." That's directly off their label. As I write this it's late September and I harvested the last of our apples, peaches, abundant nectarines, and the very last blackberries. I know what real fruit is and whatever is inside a Kellogg's Nutrigrain bar didn't look or taste like real fruit to me.

On top of a fresh peach pie, I put whipped cream from a can. The label says "real cream." It wasn't as good as freshly whipped cream, but it was pretty good. But you should see all the other stuff listed on the label just to enable this real cream to squirt out of the can.

For lunch one afternoon we prepared a healthy, oriental pork stir fry and topped it off with crunchy fried onions out of a bag. French's onion crisps. Very tasty. Guess what it says on the package? Real Onions. Thank goodness they were real onions because I'd hate to think I was ingesting slices of silicone or silly putty.

Fewer and fewer ingredients in food grow on trees or in the ground. Increasingly, they are grown in beakers in laboratories.

Imagine this, on your next trip to the grocery store you notice a new approach: "This product uses only the finest artificial ingredients." It's not appetizing but it is honest.

We vacationed in New York City a couple of years ago and were reminded of all the illegal bootlegging of consumer goods on Manhattan streets. Fake Rolex watches; fake Gucci bags; fake jewelry.

I watched a documentary film about forged paintings by the masters, Monet, Vermeer, Rembrandt, and others. Museums and curators, along with the auction houses and the wealthy patrons who buy art, have resorted to x-rays, spectrography, and other high-tech solutions to verify authenticity of these masterpieces. Even experts are frequently fooled by fakes.

Artificiality is all around us in the food we eat, the news we consume, the Botox we inject in our faces, the implants and whitened teeth in our mouth, hair extensions on heads, face lifts, plumped lips and cheekbones. I don't have a single pair of pants made from natural fibers. Not one. And I prefer these new, lightweight fabrics to cotton and wool. Hang a sign around my neck: "Imposter." "Fraud." "Fake." "Wool Hater." "Sheep Lives Matter."

Using "real" ingredients makes a lot of sense. As you know "Choosy mothers choose Jif." There are increasing numbers of choosy mothers. Millions of consumers are demanding safer, healthier, foods and it's a smart business decision to help us all understand the dangers of "bio-engineered" food stuffs. The US Government is stepping up efforts to ensure that consumers know, in simple terms, what goes into the stuff we eat, what goes into our collective mouths. We have a long, long way to go, but generally speaking, things are changing for the better.

I'm wondering if there might be a way to create a list human of ingredients. Let's require every person to have a label of ingredients on their back. The list might include: Honest. Cooperative. Funny. Hard working. Kind and caring. Claims to have a five handicap in golf but lies about his shots and fakes his score card.

This approach would have advantages. Let me illustrate.

A group of guys, malingering somewhere, see a pretty girl walk by. One of them might say, "Look at that blonde. Man has she got curves. (This is a mild, PG version of what men think and say.)

These same men, now, better informed with a label of ingredients, might respond this way: "Oh, look at her. She has real integrity." The others in the group may point out her kindness factor, "60% of the daily recommended amount."

Imagine a group of women drooling over a handsome fire fighter. "Look at those biceps. He could pull me out of a fire any day. (Do women really check out biceps. What is it women look for?)

Now, under the new labeling laws, the girls might look at the same fire fighter and say, "Oh look he has a very good track record for rescuing cats. He has a tender side." Or, "He also has real sincerity. It's hard to find a good man like that. He is so real."

ALL THE LONELY PEOPLE . . .

WHERE DO THEY ALL

COME FROM?

Paul McCartney and John Lennon

DARNING SOCKS IN THE NIGHT

Eleanor Rigby
Picks up the rice in the church
*   where a wedding has been,*
Lives in a dream.
Father McKenzie, darning his socks
*   in the night when there's nobody*
*   there.*
What does he care?
All the lonely people,
Where do they all come from?
All the lonely people
Where do they all belong?

This may be the saddest song in rock and roll history. A song of the lonely and sad. The entire decade of the 60s was as lonely and sad as it was wearying. This song, as much as any other, seems to have defined the times. For those of us who lived through that turbulent decade, and witnessed assassinations, war protests, a sexual revolution, the spawning of a drug culture, many of us felt isolated, conflicted, confused.

We are living through a new era of isolation, fatigue, turbulence, and a Covid-induced uncertainty. It's a deeply troubling time marked by angriness and shouting at each other. We'll survive. We're resilient.

I look back at the sixties with neither fondness nor regret. It was transformative, to be certain. I didn't join a protest. I didn't inhale. I didn't go to Woodstock.

But, in the 60s, I passed from childhood into adulthood, wiser for the challenges, stronger for the pain.

And my mother sat and darned socks in the night when there was nobody there.

Dad was the prototypical traveling salesman, gone much of the time. Mom would sit in front of the TV, watching the Red Skelton show, her favorite, while laboriously darning socks.

Darning socks is a lost art. Another word for "darning" is "reweaving." My mother would take a sock with a hole in the toe, put it over a round object, (you could use a light bulb for instance, or a wooden sphere from a craft store) and row by row by tedious row, sew new threads in a crosshatch pattern until the hole disappeared. She was a magician.

Four boys produced a lot of holey socks. Mom darned dozens of them weekly, a constant chore.

She attempted to use the right color thread to match the original color of the socks, but this was low on her priority list. Green thread on a blue sock never hurt, and besides, she would point out, the repair is inside your shoe where it doesn't show.

For many of those years we all wore white athletic socks, the kind with three stripes around the top, and she had plenty of white thread. The repairs, indeed, didn't show inside our high-top Chuck Taylor Converse All Star athletic shoes.

I frequently had patches on my denim jeans, patches on my socks. Sometimes it was embarrassing. Most of the time not so much. It never felt to me that we were poor, but budgets were always tight. We didn't have a lot of fancy new clothes, or shoes. We had to make things last longer.

We lived a "patchy" life.

Darning socks was one way to stretch. Mom also saved wrapping paper, and boxes full of ribbons. When I received my present on my birthday. (We got just one present, not a truckload like my grandkids get) it was wrapped in the same paper, the same box and ribbon that my younger brothers had. A month later it would be on my older brother's gift, having been carefully stored away and pressed with an iron to get wrinkles out. When opening a gift, mom would caution, "Don't tear the paper; be careful; pull the ribbon off and hand it to me." She could wrap any size package using very little tape, thus preventing rips and tears during the opening process.

We assumed this was the way it was done. Didn't everyone save and re-use wrapping paper? Didn't everyone repurpose bows and ribbons?

Tin foil was also reused at our house. Mom would take a piece of foil, cover a pan of lasagna while it cooked in the oven, serve us our favorite Italian dish, then wipe tomato and cheese bits from the foil, fold it and carefully store it in the closet, perfectly good, ready to use next week to cover shepherd's pie, or au gratin potatoes.

We were told that there were shortages of things like aluminum foil during the war and the great depression. People grew accustomed to such stretching, saving, re-using. As kids in the 60s, we were glad to do our part to support the war effort which was, by then, twenty years in the rearview mirror.

We lived a tin-foil life.

Because budgets were always tight, I had just two pair of shoes, one for school, the other for church. They were frequently too small, too tight for a growing kid, but I wore them without complaint.

Over the years I've had any number of shoes with holes in soles. A piece of cardboard cut from an empty cereal box, placed down inside the shoe, kept water out for a week or two, but did nothing to fix the hole, growing as if infected with a flesh-eating bacterium. There actually used to be shoe repair shops on main street, in the malls, pretty much all over town, a once thriving business. The most common repair was either a half sole or a new heel. The cobbler would take a piece of leather and glue/sew it on over the hole in your shoes, making them good for another hundred miles or so. A rubber cap on the heel would give new life to the shoes as well. The shoes always came back from the shop with a professional shine, looking not quite as good as new, but good enough to not be embarrassed.

We lived a half-soled life.

We now live far more extravagantly. I use four large pieces of heavy-duty aluminum foil when I cook baby back ribs on my smoker. Four sheets, and I toss them all away. My mother would have apoplexy.

Here's another example. In a closet, used just for such things, we have two very large plastic bins, filled with 30-40 different rolls of wrapping paper, tissue paper, three colors of cellophane, 8-10 colorful gift bags, roughly a dozen large rolls of ribbon, four or five rolls of tape, three pair of scissors, and another box or two filled to the brim with baubles and bangles, little kitschy things that get attached to a package, carefully coordinated with the season or the event.

Yes, we live extravagantly. I'm not quite Imelda Marcos, the wife of the deposed dictator, notorious for hundreds of pairs of shoes while her Filipino citizens went shoeless, but I am, nevertheless, guilty of shoes-iness. (A new word that means excessive silliness.) I don't have an actual count, but I admit to having multiple pairs of shoes, one pair for different uses. If you were to guess that I have more than thirty pair of shoes you would be close. There's one reason I don't have more than that: I have nowhere to put any more because my wife has double that many shoes and has taken up all the closet space.

Now let me say this, in Jill's defense. She is thrifty in her own way. She is a wonderful seamstress and when the grandkids have a favorite skirt that needs the hem raised or lowered, or a pair of pants is too large in the waist, grandma is a whiz at repairs/adjustments. Most of the pants I wear need adjustment in the length, normally thirty-one inches in a world of size thirty-two-inch, off-the-rack inseams. She also makes quilts, a touch of hand-made, old-fashioned comfort, and she is busily making thirteen of them, one for each grandchild. There's a touch of old-school frugality in Jill's world. And there will be a touch of grandma's warmth as each child begins leaving home.

We are frugal in other ways. As an homage to the Al Gore carbon offset fiction, the big lie, this summer we bottled beets, beans, peaches, nectarines, berries and about three dozen quart bottles of dill pickles. And we cut young corn off the cob and stacked two dozen bags of it in the freezer. We love this homemade old-fashioned goodness straight from the garden. We love the freshness. We love the taste of August sun on cold December days. And we have a greater appreciation for those throw-back days, patches-on-jeans days, rewoven socks, those years when our parents saved and scrimped and sacrificed and sewed and stretched and went without. Darning socks in the night.

The brightness of our extravagance suddenly dimmed the day the deadly Covid virus rolled into town. Toilet paper topped the list of scarcity. We were stunned by the sudden disruption, offended that we had to wait in line or get by without certain things. It felt like the frugal fifties again and I could hear my mother whisper, "Saving tin-foil wasn't such a bad idea after all." I wondered if darning socks was somewhere in my future.

This is the lingering lesson of Covid: Abundance is fleeting. Everyone is equal in the eyes of a monster.

It took the terror of a pandemic to remind me that we are not wealthy, but we are blessed. We are not intentionally wasteful, but sometimes unwise. We still throw away foil after one use. We don't have a fortune, but we are fortunate. We aren't rich but we live rich, full lives. We don't have everything, but we have all that we need.

I haven't had a pair of shoes repaired in more than fifty years. Cobblers and shoe repair shops are all gone, but if you're like me, you can still smell the inside of a shoe repair shop, the air redolent of leather, glue, polish, and second chances. And the promise of a few extra miles, a few extra months with your favorite shoes, well worn, re-soled, and still the most comfortable.

INSIDE OUT

news article from Fox News caught my eye recently. It was a very short human-interest story with a happy ending, just what I needed. It was a respite from TV news where you get the feeling that their ratings are won by rantings.

News reports about the Covid virus have been confusing and contradictory. There are days when no one seems to have the truth, only exaggerated versions of the facts, politicized and plundered for public display. So this quirky little story brightened my day.

Here's the quick version: A woman in Kentucky bought a wedding dress online. When it arrived in the mail she opened it, tried it on, looked in the mirror and had a pre-wedding, Vesuvian eruption. It was a mess. It didn't fit. It didn't look anything like the dress she ordered.

When something like this happens there is only one thing to do: yell at the manufacturer in a mean, confrontational post on Facebook, or a Twitter firebomb. This seems to be the new thing--getting angry and venting frustrations in public forums. That's what this woman did. She was furious. She sent the company a very nasty email, along with a photo of herself in the dress, and posted it so all her friends could share her tragedy.

The company that made the dress responded: "You put the dress on inside out, please put it on the right way."

Whoops.

The woman apologized, wore the dress, and we all wish her well in her new marriage. We can forgive her angry rant. It was her wedding, after all, a time when things get a little tense. But it's also a cautionary tale about letting emotions get away from you. About mean-spiritedness online. About speaking before thinking, or using social media as a platform for revenge.

Her dress was inside out. Curiously so were her emotions, on display for all the world to see. Her aggravation and angst flowed out like a toxic oil spill that pollutes the water and kills wildlife. Hard to clean up a mess like that. Hard not to be aggravated. Hard to take back nasty words spoken in haste.

A few years ago, Pixar made a movie called *Inside Out,* a witty look inside the brain of a young woman who is conflicted and angry. We see her emotions acted out by different characters, different voices in her head. Sometimes her emotions are in control, other times not so much. This clever story helps us better understand different kinds of emotions and how they control us, dominate us if we let them.

"Don't be afraid to let your emotions show." This is the new, generational advice to men who notoriously hold emotions inside, bottle them up. It's a time when men are encouraged to be in touch with their softer side. But this is hard to do. Men are tough, rugged, resilient, and we don't cry, and we don't fall apart, and we don't let little things bother us. And, speaking for men everywhere, we are still puzzled when tears come to our eyes, when emotions unexpectedly wash over us.

Be patient with us. We are trying to get the hang of it, turning our emotions inside out.

When we all saw Michael Jordan, the legendary NBA basketball player, win his first championship, we saw a very different side of this superstar. During the post-game celebration in the locker room, he held the trophy against his face and cried tears of joy. Sobbed uncontrollably. On national TV. It was a watershed moment as men everywhere witnessed this sports icon, this uber-competitive athlete, turn inside out. This was an additional fanning of the flames that fueled the national passion: "I want to be like Mike."

Don't tell anyone, but men are softer than they let on. Occasionally. There is nothing more heartwarming than seeing a great big guy pick up a newborn infant, wrap the child in his strong arms, kiss the baby's cheeks, and then completely fall apart, knees buckle, tears come flooding out as he unashamedly, unabashedly falls in love with his tiny, new offspring. Men melt. Men collapse. Men come undone. From time to time, men do turn inside out.

It happened to me when my only son was born. Emotions I had never experienced, never thought possible, came pouring out of me like a tsunami wave, flooding the delivery room floor. My insides were out.

In one of the most beautiful songs ever recorded, Tony Bennett croons, "I left my heart in San Francisco." What a great lyric, a powerful way to say you are inside out, letting your heart tell the story of people and places that moved you; your tales of being lost and found; hope and heartache; breaking and healing; fear and courage.

I don't have a spreadsheet with an accurate number, but of late I have caught myself counting all the times I've left my heart, left a small piece of it, here and there, with people and events that influenced me, relationships that shaped me, opportunities that strengthened me, lifted me, improved me. It's a very big number.

I have always been, and continue to be a "tough guy," macho, strong and firmly in control. It's what men do, not simply by choice but by genetic predisposition. But I have become increasingly comfortable with letting my emotions flow, letting my insides hang out, increasingly grateful to be a man who can admit defeat at the hands of hardships and human emotions. Tears more readily flow these days, but they are not signs of weakness, they are the proud wailings and warblings of a seventy-year old man, the drippy, messy, snot of a septuagenarian, the liquid passion of an aging man who is proud to be a puddler, increasingly dazzled, amazed and deeply touched by the smallest of things, the tiniest of miracles, the wonder of children, the power of family ties, the changing of seasons, the turning of a page, tender touches and tender mercies.

And while emotions aren't always measured in tears alone, it does seem to me that tears are rewards for passion, an outward display of truth, a never-ending wellspring of living water flowing from deep inside our inner soul.

I laughed at the story of the woman and the near disaster of her wedding dress. I loved her openness and her public apology. I loved the lesson of the dress: Be slow to anger, slower to show anger in public forums, avoid hasty judgments until you make sure your dress is on the right way.

Careful, you may have it on inside out.

A GOOD SYCAMORE

I once had a neighbor who was a little off-kilter. Forget all that "love your neighbor" sentiment. This guy was strange—a combination of a high-strung poodle and a buzz saw. Noisy. Nervous. Twitchy. He talked very loud and didn't take very good care of his yard. For the most part, he kept to himself, thankfully, because I didn't like to go out if he was around. Conversations with him always lead to redneck disagreements over trivial things. Let's just say, he didn't bring out the best in me.

It all started with poplar trees. Along the property line that divided our lots he planted a line of Lombardy poplars. And he didn't ask my opinion or permission, even though they were on his property and didn't need my permission. Poplars are fast-growing trees and within two years we had a dandy screen between our homes that also served as a windbreak. I'll admit that the idea of trees forming a wall between him and me had a lot of appeal, but because poplars grow fast, they also die fast because they are very brittle.

A good maple or sycamore will last a hundred years, maybe more. A lucky poplar will make it to twenty years, maybe. It's my opinion that when building a neighborhood, the long-term interests should be considered.

Better yet, heed the advice of the poet Robert Frost: "Good fences make good neighbors."

Trees weren't our only barrier. One afternoon, after a grueling commute on a hot August day, I longed to drag myself into my home and head for the nearest pitcher of pink lemonade. Mr. Poplar next door had something else in mind.

"Hey Hurst, come here," he shouted.

Oh, no! What does he want?

"You've got to see this. Come on."

Don't get between me and pink lemonade on hot days, and don't give me orders, I was tempted to say. He didn't see me roll my eyes as I followed him. I leaned forward over the galvanized steel window well.

"That's the biggest rat I ever seen," he said. "You ever seen a rat that big, Hurst? Geez! I've never seen anything that ugly."

"No." I replied. Then with a smug smile on my face, I explained that the animal in his window well wasn't a rat. As fate would have it, I had been in this situation before and knew it was a muskrat. Muskrats do, indeed, look like big rats: nose, tail, ears—the whole bit. But they are the size of a cat and spooky-looking creatures. They prowl around at night and this fellow, like the one I met years ago, had fallen into the window well by accident (they're near-sighted and nocturnal) and couldn't get out.

"What should we do?" he asked.

"What do you mean "we"?"

"Well, you're the expert."

"I'm not an expert," I said. "I've just seen one before."

"Then I'm calling the cops."

"The cops?" I asked. "What will they do? Arrest him for trespassing? Let's call animal control. They generally deal in dogs and cats, but let's call them."

Animal control sent a cop. He was on the small side, not a big hulking prototypical cop. He came into the backyard armed to the teeth with a revolver, handcuffs and a nightstick.

"What? No straight-jacket?" I kidded. "Are you going to give him a Breathalyzer test?"

My comment about the straitjacket nearly got me in one.

"It's a muskrat," the officer said. "They wander around at night and can't see to walk. This happens quite a bit." I gloated. "Go get two paper grocery bags and stuff one inside the other. And hurry."

"Aren't you going to shoot him?" Mr. Poplar asked.

"No. We'll take him alive," the officer said.

I laughed through my nose and muttered "you'll have a hard time putting handcuffs on his short little legs." They both glared at me. This was very serious business.

Turns out the police officer raised snakes as a hobby. When we made the call to animal control, he had heard about it on the radio and asked to go. This muskrat would feed his boa constrictor for a month.

"A boa won't eat a dead animal," the officer said.

"I know that." I was about to be ill. Imagine a snake swallowing a whole, furry rodent the size of a cat. Ugh!

My neighbor soon returned with the grocery bags.

Quick as cat, the cop jumped down into the window-well, nightstick drawn, Gary Cooper high-noon stance. Face to face with a hissing muskrat. Moving slowly, he placed the tip of the stick directly above the animal's head (remember, muskrats are near-sighted) and with a sudden lunge, thumped the beast right between the eyes, knocking him out as cold as a cucumber. BAM!

"Give me the sack. Quick! This is going to be one mad muskrat when he comes to." In one motion the intruder was in the bag and the cop was out of the window well, running to his car. With sirens blaring, he was off to the snake den.

My neighbor and I looked at each other as though we had been hit between the eyes with a nightstick. We were stunned. The smooth efficiency of our peewee public defender was impressive.

"A muskrat?" he asked.

"A muskrat," I said. And he wondered where I had previously seen one. Then he asked a few more questions and soon we were chatting, and soon we were having lemonade and, after that, the conversations never stopped. We shared insights about lawn fertilizer, weed control, raising kids, his blue-collar view of world politics. I no longer had just a neighbor with obnoxious trees, I had a new friend.

We moved from that neighborhood sometime later and I haven't seen or talked to Mr. Poplar since. The tale of arresting a muskrat has been repeated ad nauseum. My wife can almost quote it verbatim I've told it so many times, each telling with a little more color and a few more exaggerations. People are spell bound when I talk about this comedy of errors and they all want to know if the cop got home in time; did the snake eat the whole thing; how long did it take for the boa constrictor to finish the muskrat off?

I don't know. I didn't follow up with any of that. I have no idea about any of it. Strangely no one has ever asked, "Do you and the neighbor still talk—are you still friends?" Most people ignore all that, far more curious about the fate of the rodent.

We now live in an area carved out of a hillside, and our farmland, to date, is muskrat free. I can now overlook the valley—a perspective I like. I'm still planting flowers and nurturing lawns, showing off my unmatched skills at yard care. I'm comfortable with my surroundings and I like to think I am safe from a near-sightedness that may lead to dark holes with no escape, and occasional sharp blows between the eyes. And I'm comfortable with my newfound wisdom about tearing down walls. Nebbish, noisy, nosey neighbors with bad trees and bad lawn might well be awaiting a good friendship.

I don't plant poplar trees and advise others against them. But I do occasionally see them here and there and admire the shade they cast, the windbreak they provide and the dense screen they form between neighbors who have messy yards. In that sense, poplar trees are a good idea if they can start a meaningful conversation about fences and trees and kind deeds and a deeper understanding of "neighbor".

Plant your fast growing Lombardy Poplar trees if you must, but, my friend, a good sycamore will last more than a hundred years, and is still a much better choice.

DUMP TRUCKS

very kind employer once who taught me a valuable lesson. While paying my own tuition in college and preparing to get married I got licensed to drive big trucks. The money was better than any other summer job. I was a horrible truck driver. I struggled with shifting the gears on a diesel dump truck and I simply have never been able to look in a rear-view mirror and back up any vehicle, especially a monstrous dump truck, the oldest in the fleet. These are about the only skills someone needs to be a dump truck driver and I had neither. I was slow and painfully inept.

One day, completely bored with it all, I dumped a big load of fill dirt at a construction site. I was somewhere between complete boredom and a deep sleep when I dumped my load, pulled ahead and forgot to put the bed of the dump truck back to the down position. It's just a simple pull of a lever but I completely forgot to pull it. As I pulled forward, the raised bed snagged a temporary power line that was providing all the electricity to the very large housing project. In one instant all drills, power saws, lighting, compressors, all the things being used by the skilled craftsmen on the site—gone. Done. Blackout. An entire chorus of cursing rose up from the skeletal frames of the houses. And some 40-50 workers, the foreman included, came running at my truck waving their arms and screaming at me.

If I had been better at shifting I would have made a run for the border but I couldn't find reverse.

The entire crew was shut down for about half a day while the power company came out and put a new line back in. Everyone on the job was working for hourly wages so the shutdown was painful and costly. The foreman didn't say a word, just pointed his enormous index finger in the direction of the yard back at the trucking company. It took me 10 minutes to find first gear, 50 workers cringing and/or laughing at the grinding of gears.

Next morning 8 am, the owner of the trucking company and I had a chat. As I walked into his office I could imagine him telling me how I had hurt a lot of people; how incompetent I was; how dangerous and reckless I had been; only boneheads would be so stupid. Mr. college boy is smarter than the rest of us? How in the world could you have been so stupid?

But, he didn't get mad, didn't even fire me. Instead he asked me if I liked driving diesel dump. "I'm getting married in two months and I decided to do it for the money," I sheepishly said.

"That's not what I asked," he replied. "Do you like driving truck? If so, let's get you some more training, some help, some mentoring from the other drivers. Let's take a couple of weeks to get you some more practice miles and make a good driver out of you. How does that sound?"

It sounded kind. It sounded fair. It sounded very much like compassion and forgiveness. He could have fired me, thrown me out in the street, made me pay for all the lost wages.

Instead of him making a final and painful judgment, he allowed me to make it. I didn't want to drive trucks for the rest of my life. One summer was quite enough. I didn't want extra training or mentoring. I knew I was a horrible driver. I didn't want to be around this very tough, blue-collar environment for even another day, much less for the rest of my working days. It was the most dreadful thing I've ever done.

But he let me reach that conclusion myself. I already knew I was in a bad place, a bad job that didn't suit me, that I had shortcomings and weaknesses. He didn't need to point out any of this to me. I knew it, and I knew that he knew it. He didn't need to be critical. He gave me an open invitation to stay on the job, to improve, to get better, to make it a good experience. He invited me to stay knowing I would choose to leave.

That vexing counsel to not judge others took on an entirely new degree of clarity that day. It came in three-part harmony:

First, it's easy to fall into the trap of criticizing, demeaning others, intolerance, racism, bigotry and hate because someone is not exactly like you. Everyone does it. It's all around us. It's easy to demean others that don't measure up to our standards without knowing what's going on in their lives. It's easy to be a judge, even one who hides behind the curtains of social media invisibility where you can anonymously hand down harsh sentences to those who have less "likes" than you.

Second, embedded in this counsel, is the concept of discernment. There are times when your instincts light up and tell you: I shouldn't be here, I shouldn't trust him or her, this feels wrong, this is not what I want. Listen to this voice.

Third, learn how to judge yourself. You can be harsh, you can be kind and loving, you can be direct. You can deploy any manner of kindness or criticism. And you can learn to listen and learn from constructive criticism. By invoking honest, self-criticism, self-improvement, you learn a lot about how to better see others around you.

In the end it's pretty basic. Treat people with fairness and an open mind. Use caution, courage, charity, consistency, patience, tolerance, and remember to lower the bed when you've finished dumping your load. There's a simple release lever in plain sight. Just give it a tug.

Better yet, stay out of big trucks.

I MAY HAVE KILLED MY FATHER

I may have killed my father.

This is a confession. It's taken a few years to find the courage to finally write it for the authorities and to all who read about this most egregious transgression, but here it is.

I haven't taken it lightly, this *meaculpa*, finally coming forward three years after his death, so that I can find some peace and move on.

I miss the old guy. He died at age 96 after living alone without my mother for about fifteen years. He was a tragic widower. He never cooked, never shopped at a grocery store, never balanced a checkbook, or paid the bills. Living alone was not the plan.

There never was a plan. Reluctantly, he consented, in his final five years, to move into an assisted living facility. It was a very good experience for him to have help always available and to have his meds and meals provided for him with regularity. He grumbled and moaned a bit about the food and all the rest, but he also made friends by the score. He was the unofficial mayor of Legacy Senior Living.

The kids and grandkids visited frequently and brightened his lonely days. He loved Almond Joy candy bars and other contraband we smuggled in on a regular basis. I stopped by one afternoon for a visit and shared with him the following story:

We had recently moved to a pretend little farm in northern Utah, and I accepted an invitation from a neighbor to go horseback riding. The mountains were awash with Fall color, aspen yellow, sumac orange, maple red. The blue-green spruce trees broke up the monochromatic palette. My host, a seasoned horse lover, walked two horses from the corral and tied them to a trailer where the saddle and tack were kept. My horse was prepared first.

On the other side of the trailer, Kendall, my friend, went about getting the second horse outfitted. He was out of view, or should I say I was out of his view. Thankfully.

Standing alongside my trusty mount, a very calm, approachable animal, I grabbed three or four apples lying on the ground and fed them to my new partner, a bribe, a token of appreciation for being willing to give me a ride. A plea for leniency. I've been told that a horse can sense fear, so I went overboard trying to be cool and calm. I called him dude and tried to take on a James Dean casual saunter, a Paul Newman smolder.

As I stood there it seemed to me that this was an unusually tall animal. Kendall assured me it wasn't. I had ridden horses, any number of times over the years, but I didn't remember them being this big. The saddle, I noticed, was sitting at exactly the top of my head. That's six feet, seventy-two inches. That's a big step up.

I decided to mount the horse to make sure I could do it without embarrassment. Kendall worked away, still out of view. The stirrup hung at about the same level as my belt line. "Just put your foot up there," I thought to myself. "You can do this. All I have to do is imitate a movie cowboy who puts his boot in the stirrup, pushes himself up, swings the other leg over, butt in saddle ready to roll." The movie cowboys have a fluid, rhythmic, effortless mount, akin to figure skater gliding on ice, backwards, etching a figure eight in the ice. Smooth and graceful.

There would be no grace. There would be no fluidity. I looked again at the stirrup, hanging there, roughly belt high. I struggle to put my socks on every morning and can't lift my leg high enough to do even that simple task. How can I possibly get my foot into a stirrup that high?

I leaned into the horse for stability, then grabbed my left foot and started pulling and tugging trying to get my shoe (running shoes, not boots) into the leather stirrup. My leg doesn't go that high, hasn't for thirty years. My foot wouldn't bend to the correct angle. My knees groaned. This is a very bad way to start a horseback ride. I couldn't get on the horse.

As I told the story, Dad sat there enthralled and began to chuckle. His grin, a wise-old-man smirk looked like he knew what was coming. His brand-new dentures glistened, the straight, white teeth taking ten years off his leathery face.

I got up out of my chair and began acting out the rest of the story. How would Buster Keaton play this scene?

After a dozen attempts, I finally got my foot in the stirrup, ready to swing my leg around. Now I want to quickly insert here that I had two semesters of Physics in school. I got a C-minus both terms, saved from failure because I took an extra-credit field trip to Hill Air Force Base with the JETS, our high-school Physics club, populated by geeks, nerds, and various other Middle Earth creatures with pocket protectors and well-worn copies of *The Lord of the Rings* always in their backpacks. I apparently failed the section on torque and/or leverage. I couldn't calculate how to get on the horse without a ladder. The shame would be too much. My macho adventure simply couldn't begin with a ladder.

With my left foot in the stirrup (Did I mention it was impossibly far off the ground?) I had no possible way to push off with my right leg. The left leg was too high. I'd been on this outing for a total of about three minutes when my first cramp hit. The right hamstring tightened up while making little hops, careful not to have my foot slip out of the stirrup. Finally, a big push. Hand on the horn of the saddle, I let go a big heave, a big moan, a big fart, and jerked my other leg upward.

Completely exhausted, I had successfully moved twelve inches off the ground. Hanging on to the top edge of the saddle I knew I was going to have to pull myself onto the horse, still with zero leverage in my legs. Straining, pulling, right leg flailing, I somehow ended up horizontal, suspended, barely hanging on, sideways, nearly parallel to the ground. Then, with a giant, last ditch attempt, full force in the stirrup, and a big pull on the saddle, I did it. I was, at last, on top of the horse, on top of the saddle, technically aboard except for one tiny detail. My body was hanging over the animal like you would carry a dead body back from a gun fight. More like you would carry a bag of potatoes, feet on one side, my head on the other, the saddle cutting off my lungs. I couldn't breathe. I couldn't move. Kendall was finishing up with his horse. "I've got to get in this saddle."

A couple of deep breaths, mustering all my strength, a big push, swing the leg over, and... I did it. I was upright, sitting in the saddle atop this enormous beast. Backwards.

I paused the story. My dear old dad was red-faced, bending over, laughing uncontrollably, his mouth wide open, the silent laugh of the breathless.

"Dad, Dad, take a breath." I patted him on the back as he grabbed his side and steadied himself.

Back to the story. I was atop the horse, backward. I slowly, cautiously, pivoted around, both feet resting on the horse's butt, steady, steady, steady, BOOM. Cramp number two hits. It's in my left hip. Son of a . . . . I writhed, I winced, I tried stretching it out. I was backwards on a horse with nothing to hold on to. I grabbed on to the tail, the mane, the horse's left ear, clinging to anything I could find. Seconds away from falling off the horse, the ultimate embarrassment, I forced myself around, facing front, both feet in the stirrups, just as Kendall walked around, surprised to see me aboard already.

Kendall asked, "Wow, you're ready to go. You got aboard okay?"

"Sure, no problem," I replied with just a hint of my John Wayne impersonation, wishing I had brought a bottle of Advil with me. Kendall is ten years younger than me and has been a horse guy most of his life. He mounted his horse with a gravity-defying efficiency that would have thrilled Mr. Paulson, the 11th grade Physics teacher. (I should add that Kendall Johnson, is a real-life rocket science, very smart and knows the laws of physics, torque, timing, momentum, the pull of gravity.)

I thought a twenty-minute ride around the foothills sounded nice. Trot around a bit, see the scenery from fifteen-hands high, enjoy the cool Autumn weather. It ended up being a ninety-minute ride into the hills, and a ninety-minute ride back down.

I saw my dad's face contort. I knew his cringe, his "oh-no" shake of the head I had seen dozens of times as a teenager.

About a mile up the trail there is a small creek, mostly dry this September day, but still very muddy. Kendall said we'll have to jump it which is exactly what he and his horse did. He gave a little kick, and the horse knew exactly what to do. Like Elizabeth Taylor in Black Beauty, it was a work of art, horse and rider working together, safely across the muddy creek bed.

"HEY! Where are you going?" Kendall shouted to me.

"I'm going a little further upstream. I've got to find a spot to cross. I can't jump it."

"Sure, you can," my friend assured me. "You're not jumping it, the horse is. He knows what to do."

"No, I'll just keep looking for a better spot. I'll catch up with you."

"Mark," he said, patiently, "This is the best spot. It's narrowest right here. Trust me. Just give the horse a little kick and he'll do just fine."

I got on this animal just ten minutes earlier and I wasn't real anxious to fall off and have to re-mount. I wasn't exactly thrilled about the distinct possibility of falling off and breaking my back, either.

"And hang on tight," Kendall reminded, as if I hadn't thought of that little detail. "Let your knees act like a shock absorber."

I hung on. I hung on, desperately. My seventy-year-old knees took the blow and my thrice surgically repaired meniscus popped. My neck snapped and my jaw slammed shut with a crack, the sound of an entire box of delicate china dropping on concrete. My feet, knees, teeth, elbows all crackled the sound of brittle branches snapping off. My hamstrings knotted. My ears hurt. My toenails hurt. Everything hurt.

But I didn't fall off.

"Good job," Kendall the rocket scientist pronounced.

Even my cheeks hurt, I discovered, when I gave him the phony smile of gratitude.

Up the mountain we went, every step a jolt, every step a pile driver in rocks, every step a sledgehammer on a hundred-pound metal anvil.

Ninety minutes in we finally took a break and dismounted. The horses grazed a bit while the two riders got a beverage from the saddle bags and took in the mountain scenery, the autumn tableau.

"Kendall, I need to tell you something."

He looked worried. "Are you okay?"

"More or less," I told him. "It's just that, Well, I don't think I can get back on the horse."

"No worries. Neither can my little grandkids. Let me show you how." I'm pretty sure he just compared me to his young grandkids.

Jets alumni, (the high school physics club) take note. You're about to be schooled by a real-life rocket scientist who is going to demonstrate how to get on a horse using complex laws of physics.

"Go around to the other side." Kendall said, in a matter of fact, glaringly obvious way.

"Say what?"

He repeated the complicated, important scientific instructions. "Go to the other side."

"The right side? You want me to go to the other side? How will that help?"

"Because it has an uphill slope."

We were riding in the foothills of the mountains that surround Cache Valley in Northern Utah, one of the most beautiful spots in the entire Rocky Mountain region. Just moments away from the farm, we have climbed to seven-thousand feet on steep, rocky terrain. The trail is narrow, single file only on horseback. Using the uphill side, I effortlessly walked up the slope, nature's ladder, and virtually floated on to the saddle.

Ninety minutes still to go back down from the hills and home again. The horses intuitively knew we were heading home and wanted to run the entire way. My horse is now transformed into one of those new autonomous vehicles, driving itself, built-in GPS showing the horse the way. Jolt, jolt, jolt, jolt.

Oh, no. A sudden thought popped into my head. The creek. We have to cross that annoying creek again. My left meniscus says, "Don't even think about it." My spine is beeping like a smoke alarm going off in the middle of the night. My molars are screaming, "abandon ship."

Fortunately, I didn't have to think about jumping the creek. I didn't have to make an alternate plan. I didn't realize we had come to the creek so quickly, until slow-motion replay showed the horse, airborne, rider screaming like a little girl, mid-air over the creek. My slow-motion reaction, my split-second thought? "SSSSSSSSHHHHHHHHHHIIIIIIIIITTTTTT."

I looked at my dad. My wife was helping him sit up straight. He had fallen nearly out of his chair. His face was the color of ripe apples, not pink, not blush, but deep dark red. He was coughing, wheezing. His silent laughs drained his lungs. He can't breathe, he can't move. He is hopelessly trapped in the vise-like grips of a true, gut-busting laugh. It's a deep, painful, hysterical laugh from somewhere deep in his frail 96-year-old body, letting go a thousand laughs stored in the cellar of humor, waiting for just the right opportunity, the last great laugh, a final good-bye toast.

Jill grabbed a Coke from the tiny refrigerator, the pause that refreshes. "Finish the story," she warned, barely able to control her own hysteria.

We got down the mountain, in-tact, more or less. My inner thighs throbbed. My gloveless hands were blistered and oozing, evidence of a white-knuckle grip on the saddle horn and reins.

I helped get saddles off, and brushed my horse. I got him 4 or 5 apples and thanked him for the ride. I thanked my host.

Back home, I headed for the shower, sweaty Levi's, covered in horsehair, dropped in the laundry. I limped down the hall, the bow-legged shuffle of an aging cowboy, the Robert Duvall western waddle. I got the water as warm as I could stand. I was alive. I was about to have the best shower of my life.

I was about to have the worst shower of my life.

The warm water hit my butt. The pain in my molars immediately went away. My knees felt completely healed. My jaw, my neck, my spine, all miraculously stopped hurting the moment that warm water hit my butt. Every single receptor in my body, you know, the ones that transmit pain, turned their entire attention to my butt, and the softball-sized, open wound thereon.

I dropped to my knees and screamed, music from *Psycho* screeched as Norman Bates' knife stabbed at my bare derriere, EEH, EEH, EEH.

There is no salve for this kind of open wound. No balm. No unguent. No way to bandage it. I couldn't sleep, couldn't sit in a chair, couldn't walk, and couldn't wear pants for a couple of weeks. I mentioned to Dad that I walked around naked for a week because of the enormous hole in my butt.

More laughing, more coughing. The poor old guy was having a hard time. I had to run down to the free ice cream bar they have in the lobby of the facility and get him a large bowl of vanilla. Eventually, we left dad in a calm mood. We had a great visit.

He died a few hours later.

True story. This is not something I would joke about. Just hours after telling him the story, about 2:00 in the morning, a care giver found him unresponsive. The facility alerted my sister who called me with the grim news.

"Vicki," I said, morning hoarseness scratching out the words, "Did a doctor tell you what happened?"

"No. There was nothing. He just died in his sleep," she explained, lovingly.

"Vicki, there's something I need to tell you." She cut me off saying, "I know, we'll all have a lot to say but let's get together first thing in the morning and talk it over."

"No, no, Vicki, I have to tell you something. It's very important."

"Get some sleep. I have to call the other siblings. Collect your thoughts and we'll see you in a few hours."

"I killed him," I blurted out.

Vicki laughed, a little 2 a.m. weak laugh. "Right, I know, you're very sad. Talk to you soon."

This was going to be harder than I thought.

My father very likely died laughing. I overdid it. He couldn't breathe because I overstressed him, stretched beyond capacity his ancient lungs, and, surely, I killed my own father. I can still see his red face, hear him coughing. Feeding him ice cream likely didn't help, but he enjoyed hearing the story of my grand, painful misadventure and I was thrilled to tell it.

Next morning, I decided I wouldn't mention the murder to my siblings. It didn't seem like the right time. I wanted to listen and understand how much trouble I might be in. The doctors were certain that old age just crept in and took him away, painlessly, peacefully, the way every one of us would select if given the choice. I knew there was something else that finally ended his 97th year. I kept mum.

It took me three years, but I finally broke with Omerta, the code of silence. I was prepared to make a statement to the authorities and confess my crime. Patricide. I killed my own father. My siblings thought I was being absurd. They were jealous. They thought I was taking too much credit for mercilessly hastening his farewell from a lengthy, well-worn life. Comedy-induced euthanasia.

There was no autopsy, no investigation, the police didn't want my statement. The mortuary, the doctors, the government officials felt okay if I wanted to petition to have the official death certificate read, "Cause of death: He died laughing."

This true story happened about three years ago. I haven't been on a horse since and feel comfortable I've had my last cowboy round up. I started thinking about losing parents, missing them, as we quarantined ourselves in Covid prison, watching the news, trying, in vain, to grasp the tragic reality that millions of people around the globe were dying from complications of the Corona virus. It has been a grim time. A desperate time. Many families have found pleasure in being together in the quiet new world, forced to stay home and slow down a bit from our normally hectic lives, finding joy in small things, calming nerves, and laughing whenever possible.

We are all told, "Something is going to kill you." Based on my recent experience, euthanizing my father, it might just as well be laughter and a bowl of ice cream. This would be my first choice.

And if I get too old and feeble to carry on my mortal existence, and want to hasten my departure, I'm going to call my friend Kendall Johnson and ask him to take me on a three hour horse ride into the Utah Mountains where I can die the honorable death of a cowboy, killed by a very large animal that knew a greenhorn was aboard, and gave me my final ride into the sunset as I looked westward singing "Yippe-yi-yo-kiay." And then, I'll see my father again, and the first thing I'll say to him is, "Boy do I have a story to tell you."

MORE, PLEASE.

Charles Dickens

MORE CHICKENS PLEASE

In the movie/Broadway musical, Oliver, the central character seen holding an empty bowl asking for more porridge. The doe-eyed lad, orphaned and alone, is taken in by a band of nefarious street urchins and their pocket-picking pals. Adapted from a Dickens story, we see darkness, crime, passion, anger, jealousy, rage, you know . . . classic Dickens.

This scene, the empty bowl, is the essence of the story. People of means contrasted with orphans and the undesirables, rich vs. poor, the rejected and the dejected vs. lives of abundance and arrogance.

"More, please." The prayer of the unfortunates, and, in a strange, ironic way, the unintentionally arrogant sentiment of the affluent.

I heard this very phrase, "more, please," in a more modern setting. My back yard.

"More, please." It came up in a conversation about one of the big box retailers, but I won't mention it's actual name. For now, let's just call it Sam's Club. I discussed this issue with a neighbor whose real name I won't mention. Let's just call him Jerry Olsen.

Jerry spent an entire career in the automotive aftermarket business, a very senior manager of hundreds of retail stores and employees. He understands issues of inventory, supply and demand, and how to keep the customer satisfied. He told me the model was simple: if you run out of a part, get more.

So, it was with no small amount of consternation that Jerry went to Sam's Club to get one of their highly coveted rotisserie chickens, only to be told they were all gone for the day. It was two o'clock in the afternoon. They finished up for the day in the meat section. Done with the rotisserie. At two o'clock.

Jerry's brilliant observation: "I'm pretty sure they could get more chickens. They could also install another oven. With people standing in line, clearly there is built-in demand for more chickens."

In many instances, those rotisserie chickens are the primary reason some people go shopping at Sam's. It is for me. Jerry couldn't comprehend that Sam's, one of the largest retailers in the world, seemed unable, or unwilling, to follow the most basic, the most fundamental way of solving the most important rule of retail: get more.

Jerry and I laughed about it. We revisited economics classes we both attended that taught supply and demand. It started to sound like one of those story problems in 5th grade math: If you sell 500 rotisserie chickens each day, and there are still 500 people who would buy them if you had more, why in hell don't you buy another oven? Or two. Why don't you put on another shift of workers and keep the rotisserie rotissing. Or is it rotisserieing? Doesn't matter. Attention Sam's Club: get more chickens.

Some weeks after our grumbling about chickens, a friend called me. A friend I hadn't seen or heard from in more than 50 years. We both moved away. We both had families and got caught up in the vortices of work, family, crisis management. More crises, more twists than either of us expected when we were young men. More highs and lows than we could have imagined when we were kids, collecting empty glass soda bottles and redeeming them at the grocery store for a nickel or two. Greater challenges, heavier burdens, unexpected disappointments.

And far more abundance than we deserved.

Recently, a large group of cousins and siblings made a trek to an ancestral home in Hooper, Utah. A tiny, one room cabin, built in 1867, still stands, a monument to sacrifice by our ancestors, immigrants from England. The theme of our visit was "More." Our walk-in closet is bigger than this tiny structure that housed ten people. Their extraordinary sacrifice made our rich, abundant lives possible. We saw more, felt more, connected more with progenitors whose seeds we have so abundantly reaped.

The world has lived through a frightening pandemic, an exhausting quarantine, leaving us all with the strangest feeling of isolation and fear. We want our lives back and want to spend more time with loved ones. More time seeing the world around us.

Then, just as quickly as we started feeling hopeful, another round of misery moseyed in.

A variant of Covid mutated and started another round of illness, another round of fear and uncertainty. Then came record heat, record flooding. Then came the smoke from hundreds of forest fires, lingering for months, burning our eyes and throats, and imposing yet another sun-blocking, dismal gray curtain over our head.

We wondered if we would, forever more, live with the tumult of a planet in change. Probably. But we're getting over it and getting on with it, bouncing back with the rubber resilience of human nature.

And then came autumn, just as we knew it would, a respite, a season of change.

In all the darkness, we found more light. And we found it because we needed it. Because we looked for it. Because we recognized the light when we saw it.

After the peril came promise. After the struggle came strength. After the gloom came goodness. After the isolation came inspiration. After the lows came lift.

When we all took off our masks, we saw more smiles on more faces than we've ever seen before. A smile is an easy thing to take for granted. No more.

These recent experiences, and others, made me think about the empty bowl of Oliver Twist, whose simple plea was "more." That empty bowl wasn't just about more porridge, but it was about hunger. It symbolized what Oliver craved most: love. He was starving for human affection. And I thought of my own bowl, filled to the brim with the fall harvest, filled to the brim with joy, filled to overflowing with gladness, goodness, generosity. Filled, completely with love. Filled with gratitude. My cup runneth over.

The word "more" is often thought of as a synonym for "greed." "Materialism" is another form of the sentiment. I don't see it that way. I see the word "more" in a whole new light. It now suggests our collective quest for more of the things we didn't know we've been missing.

Now if we can just find a way to help Jerry get more chickens. It's not that hard.

ON THE ROPES

I was recently diagnosed with Parkinson's disease. This is a very personal matter and no one really wants to ever read about another person's illnesses so I don't want to dwell on my diagnoses. Nor do I want to ramble on about all the things the disease has taught me so far. I don't know what it may yet teach me—I'm just rolling along in the early stages, waiting to see what's around the next corner.

One of the ways to deal with the symptoms and changes in your body, is to stay very active. I'm trying to do this. In researching this incurable malady, I discovered that many people who have PD are finding some success with the sport of boxing. Yes, boxing--putting on gloves and learning to move arms and legs, improve hand/eye coordination, and, at least as far as I'm concerned, making the punching bag into my PD opponent and punching the crap out of it to ease my frustrations.

It's a fun workout even though it tests your strength, stamina, and, the toughest part of Parkinson's, remembering what you learned just 30 seconds ago.

It's a strenuous, physical workout and it's a mental workout as well, the combination of which, provides a therapeutic reprieve three days a week.

I grew up around boxing so it was a natural fit for me. My father and my grandfather loved boxing and we spent a lot of time watching a variety of bouts. We followed the career of Gene Fullmer, a champion fighter from right here in Utah. He was a bit of a local sensation.

We also followed the careers of some of the very best pugilists, in some historic clashes, including the Olympics where Cassius Clay burst onto the scene. (He would later change his name to Muhammad Ali and would die—no small coincidence—from complications of Parkinson's disease.)

When I was about 14 years old Dad bought me some gloves and a punching bag and I loved hitting that thing. I was a very small kid and boxing made me feel bigger and tougher.

Steve Reese was a neighborhood kid who sparred with me one summer day. He took a wild swing that connected with my head and it knocked me right on my rear end. One punch. I learned a lot that day about keeping your guard up, protecting your face.

Conversely, when I took on another friend, I landed a very solid right hook and my friend's knees buckled, his legs turned to jello, and went down. He wasn't unconscious but he saw those little birdies that cartoons depict flying around your head.

I didn't pursue boxing very much after that. The gloves wore out and the punching bag turned to mush. I didn't follow the sport much either. I grew to dislike the violence and the hypocrisy of one sport (football) taking on dangerous concussions, and another sport, which thrives on them.

I vehemently abhor the idea of two women fighting. I'm old fashioned and I know it. But two females fighting simply doesn't jibe with my personal creed of honoring and respecting womanhood.

After my boxing career, the teenage crush I had on the sport, I simply turned my attention to other sports, to school, to girls, and it left no time for boxing. Then 6 months ago I got reacquainted with it.

I've been thinking a lot about this pastime, this regimen of moving, ducking, slipping a hit, and memorizing punch sequences with your gloves. We don't hit others in our class; rather we hit big, heavy bags or our coach's big mitts. Along the way, it occurred to me that we all use boxing terminology on a regular basis. Everyone knows the terms but may not readily connect them with boxing. Here are a few.

KNOCK SOME SENSE INTO HIM

Clearly this isn't a sport for the faint of heart. It's two people hitting each other until one is on their back, or injured, or has wobbly knees and has to quit. It's a brutal sport from which this aphorism comes. It's a threat, really. It means I'm mad at someone and I'm going to, figuratively, smack him until he does his job right.

I'LL BOX HIS EARS

I'm familiar with this one, not from my boxing class, but from my little 5'2" mother who was as tough as nails. Do something wrong and she would threaten to box our ears, which means you're in trouble. She never hit any of her children, as far as I know, but the threat was always there.

YOU SCORED A BIG KNOCKOUT PUNCH

Of course this means that one of the boxers won the match by pounding the opponent until he is unconscious, or can't go on. This sounds violent, and it is. In the game of football, protecting against concussions is the new number one priority. In boxing, a knock out is the ultimate goal. Sometimes it takes just one punch to connect your glove with the face of your challenger, and knock him out. Fight over.

How do we use this expression? This may mean your presentation went very well. You won the bid. You beat the competition. You closed a big deal. You got promoted to VP. You endured chemotherapy. You've beaten an addiction. You're a winner. Fight over.

ON THE ROPES

A boxing ring used to be round but now they are square, surrounded by ropes. If a guy is really whipping your behind your tendency is to run away. You do this by backing up. When you do, you run into the ropes on the edge and your opponent has you cornered. The ropes now pin you in where your opponent can continue punching you. You're in big trouble.

I had many employees over the years who had varying degrees of talent and, what you would call people skills— or a lack thereof. Some had a horrible work ethic. Others simply couldn't handle the pressures of the job and stressed out over meeting a deadline and staying on budget. On any number of occasions I realized that their skill set didn't match our needs so I had to have a talk with them about these concerns. They immediately feet that their job was on the ropes. Which it was.

SAVED BY THE BELL

When the bell rings in boxing it means your three-minute round is over, go to your corner and clean up your face. If one of the fighters is pummeling his opponent, putting him in some real trouble, the fighting, mercilessly, stops for one minute, enabling you to regroup, catch a breath, stop a cut from bleeding, start again.

I had a big presentation to make on one occasion, the biggest I'd ever done—a $50 million contract was at stake. We had a team of 5 people each doing their portion of the pitch. We had 30 minutes in front of the potential client, and my team members all talked way too long despite weeks of practicing and rehearsals. It was my turn with one minute remaining. I'm the heavyweight, the title-holder, my name is on the door and I've got 60 seconds to close this deal. We were on the ropes. (See above.) Time ran out and the client, literally, rang a bell.

Fortunately, there was an additional 20 minutes for questions and answers, and one of the members on the panel recognized my awkwardness and did a miraculous thing. I had never met her but she did me a huge favor by asking the first question in such a way that I could take 6 to 8 minutes answering. I got my time back, I rocked the presentation, and we won the $50 million deal. Saved by the bell. (Later a few of my employees felt like they were on the ropes when I chewed them out for taking too much time in the presentation.)

THROW IN THE TOWEL

The guy who sits in the corner of the ring and mops sweat off the brow of his fighter, the trainer, usually can be seen with a messy, bloody towel around his neck. The towel helps to dry up some sweat and cool the fighter down, but it is also a tool of surrender. Think white flag in battle. The manager sees his guy getting trashed and tosses the towel into the ring signifying, "We give up." Is this an act of cowardice? Generally not. What it means is, simply, a fighter was over matched and his, health, sometimes even his life is at stake. The wise manager is telling his guy, "We are walking away so we can live to fight another day. (By the way, that's another boxing term that people use all the time when odds are against them, "Live to fight another day.")

In the business world you may frequently throw in the towel on trying to close a big deal. It's just not going to happen and you walk away because it's costing you money and resources which you'll never recoup. You may get rid of a client who simply isn't making you money. You may have an employee who seemed a good fit at first, but ultimately has to move on, throw in the towel.

HE'S SUCH A LIGHTWEIGHT

This one is pretty simple. Boxers fight opponents who are in their same weight class. You wouldn't want a light weight (probably around 135 pounds) fighting a great big 240-pound heavy weight with much more strength, size, and power.

Unfortunately, business sometimes works this way. A real heavyweight is a shrewd, tough, well-trained professional who you can always count on to develop new sales channels, find new markets, that sort of thing. Some years ago I won a new piece of business by adding such a person. I doubt very much I could have managed this account without the help of a top-notch team member-- a real heavyweight.

Lightweight is clearly a derogatory term we sometimes use to rank associates, and classify them for further assignments. It's rude. But it's an apt description.

HE HAS A GLASS JAW

In boxing it means someone who isn't very good because if you connect with his jaw on a sweeping right hook, you can knock him down easily. Many boxers get a reputation of being easy to defeat because they can't take a punch.

In a modern world it means someone who is sensitive, can't take criticism, easily pushed around. You don't want a weak person on your sales team who can't meet new quotas, and help grow the business.

The list goes on. Someone hits you with a one/two punch. A cancer patient is fighting for his life. A married couple is wrestling with a tough decision about their careers. Your noisy neighbors had a knock down/drag out fight. Roll with the punches, means hanging in there despite ups and downs. Hitting below the belt, may be a person who gets personally offensive, mean, dirty. Taking off the gloves, also a dirty, bare-knuckle brawl, frequently with hostile, mean-spirited invective. Come out swinging, meaning being aggressive from the start. Duking it out may be two politicians debating an issue. Pulling punches means holding back, being timid, afraid to make a decision. Having someone in your corner who is always supporting you, protecting you.

There's more, but I'll stop. You get the idea.

Boxing isn't a complicated sport. Winning usually comes down to two factors: Who survived. And who landed the most hits. Unless there is a knockout, judges rate the performances, like gymnastics, and turn in a score sheet. There is no final score in boxing like there is in baseball or basketball, just a judge's decision.

I'm not in "fighting shape" just yet as I prepare to take on a major health challenge. "Fight ready" means training hard, getting in shape, and preparing to face your opponent. Think Rocky Balboa drinking a glass full of raw eggs and chasing a chicken. I know my opponent and I'm getting in shape a little every day. My physical and my mental well being seem to be in balance somewhat as I work and train. I've had fights before and expect to have many more. I've stood in a ring and absorbed punches before, and so have you.

No one gets through this life without trials, pain, suffering, losing a job, debilitating health problems, family strife, broken relationships, an untimely death of a friend, and other vile, vicissitudes that vex us. And make us want to throw in the towel. Problems will always be around to pummel us and knock some sense into us.

In my youth, pretending to be a pugilist was fun. Dad would come down and watch me punch on occasion. As we talked he quietly, without fanfare or drum roll, told me what he thought of fighting. He had a brother who was a brawler; a guy who drank too much, talked too much, and was frequently fighting guys for money, for fun, for recreation, or for no reason at all other than a hot temper. Dad said his brother won most of the fights but did, on occasion, hobble away, his face looking like an overstuffed bag of Idaho potatoes, swollen face, crooked nose and cuts from his forehead to his chin.

Dad would counsel me about staying out of fights. He would say, "You win 100% of the fights you never have." He liked teaching me how to hit, along with instructions to never, ever hit another person. I was puzzled. "Then why am I learning how to punch if I never use it?" I would ask. Dad's answer: "There's power in having the confidence to know you can hit someone hard. It's the confidence that makes you powerful—not the hitting."

Confidence. Courage. Hope. These are all the things you reach for when you have a tough fight. I've had family and friends fight battles with cancer and heart disease, many of whom lost their high-stakes fight. I've recently had to step into a ring I wasn't prepared for. It's throwing some serious blows but I'm gaining more confidence every day.

You, too, have stepped, perhaps, many times, into

a ring of uncertainty, fear, doubt. You may have faced trauma, turbulence, and tears. You may have found yourself "on the ropes,< ready to throw in the towel. Every single person on the planet has, or will have, title fights against world-champions. Against heavyweights more powerful than you. Keep up the good fight.

Hit a punching bag, occasionally, to take out some frustrations, but know that it's confidence that makes you strong. Be wise. Be safe. Be courageous. And stay off the ropes.

Better yet, stay out of the ring.

THINK SMALL

In 1959 a new German car was introduced to America. An American ad agency was tasked with the tough job of getting Americans to buy it. It was small. It was foreign. It was ugly. But the marketing effort effectively shifted attitudes. In my industry this is sometimes thought of as the greatest ad campaign in history. It changed a lot of minds, and Volkswagen sold a bunch of cars. I worked for this agency for a time (many years later, of course,) and I recently recalled these ads. They started me thinking about the concept of thinking small.

I was a small kid. I didn't mind it too much. My friends were always bigger than me and even my two younger brothers were taller. I didn't resent my brothers' very large frames, we got along and still get along, and enjoy a solid brother/friend relationship. They are big men.

Old aunts and uncles would always tell me, "Good things come in small packages." I grew weary of this notion, thinking that it sounded more like pity than affirmation. But I accepted my fate and ultimately started believing the advice of these septuagenarian sages, hoping for good things, hoping for a few more inches.

I don't know the origins of this phrase, "Good things come in small packages," but somewhere along the way it got co-opted by Tiffany's, the New York jewelry store, famous for their little blue boxes. If someone gives you a little blue box for a gift, you can be sure it's a good thing.

Charlie Brown, the sad little boy from the *Peanuts* cartoon series, picked out a Christmas tree that was undersized. When he took it home most of the needles fell off the tree and his friends had a good laugh. Charlie Brown described the tree as "small but sincere."

One of my peach trees struggled this year with record breaking heat and drought and produced undersized peaches. I called them "Charlie Brown peaches," small but sincere. About half the size of peaches from my other tree, the fruit was every bit as sweet and juicy as their larger cousin. Just smaller.

In 1915, or close to that year, my maternal grandfather built and operated a small general store in Hooper, Utah. It was a good business for a time, prosperous enough that he was able to build a nice home in the small town. He also had the first automobile in the area.

Each summer there would be an Independence Day parade in downtown Hooper, a little community right on the shores of The Great Salt Lake. To boost business, Grandpa told his oldest son, Claude, to make a sign promoting the store, and join the parade. Claude followed orders and hand-painted a sign on a piece of fabric draped over his horse. He rode in the parade, proud of his hard work. The sign read:

C.G. PARKER'S GENERAL STORE

Small but efficient.

Who would have guessed? Advertising was in my genes. This isn't the best tagline I've heard but it was genuine.

It didn't work.

Customers, during these very hard years, were given credit in the store. Get what you need and pay for it when you can. C.G., that's what he was called, was far too generous, far too forgiving, and was slow to collect payments. The store struggled to make any money. The business was in trouble.

Then came the advent of the automobile. Then came Henry Ford who made cars affordable to everyone. In a very short time, everyone in Hooper had a car and started driving to Ogden, or even Salt Lake City, to do their shopping. C.G. Parker's General Store teetered and wobbled. The new slogan might well have been, "Small but foolish."

Family diaries and journals are a little vague, but around 1923 or 24, Grandpa closed the store for good and turned to farming in Burley, Idaho. My mother would tell me stories of the farm and described it as "small but sufficient." This was her way of saying it was a rough time. All eight kids left the farm as soon as they could. They put small farms, small towns and small times in rear view mirrors and never returned.

This is my heritage: small but sufficient.

I grew up, finally reached six feet in height, got the girl of my dreams. Together we walked on some significant stages, basked in the glow of some significant lights, met and socialized with many prominent people. We have loved and appreciated our "big" opportunities.

Now that the klieg lights have dimmed, I celebrate small things in my life. I've found that klieg lights can make you look pale, washed out. I celebrate the small moments of delight and pleasure, small inspirations. They are countless.

All of us have big events in our lives, weddings, babies, success in business, getting accepted to a prestigious college, getting the big job offer. And there are far too many sad events, miseries, plagues, families falling apart, bodies aging and rusting, prolonged illnesses, unexpected deaths. There will always be big things in our lives. Catastrophes. Explosions that rock our worlds. Angry volcanoes.

And pandemics.

I have discovered that when all the catastrophic dust and debris have settled, I can see more clearly the small things that made a big difference for good. In the end it's always the small things that matter the most. Good people, good friends, small moments of joy and delight. Small things survive.

When our family gets together, we rarely sit around and argue about petty things. There is very little of sibling rivalries and family friction. We have endless conversations that frequently begin and end with this sentiment: "Remember the time?" And they are always small little moments, silliness, goofiness, the songs we sang in the car, our nicknames for each other, fish soup in Norway, a smelly starfish in a warm car, the dog that pooped out a red foil wrapper of a Hershey's chocolate kiss, and fair-weather snorkeling. Trust me, these are hilarious. In our family small is good. We celebrate the momentous but keep coming back to the less momentous. We remember the mountains and rejoice in the mole hills.

All of us find happiness in these small moments of delight. Every brain comes pre-wired with a pleasure center that keeps track of things, and fires and refires synapses of pleasure and happiness. We are wired to have joy.

Your small moments may include the friend who stood by you, the colleague that defended you, the teacher who encouraged you, the wounded soul who forgave you, the preacher who inspired you, the employer who believed in you, a loving partner who stayed with you. Anyone who whispers in your ear, "Job well done."

The Pandemic has been a volcanic eruption. It covered us all in the Vesuvian ash of fear, uncertainty, and doubt as we were forced to self-quarantine. But we didn't huddle in our homes and tremble. We found small ways to celebrate being alive, to rejoice in togetherness. Small moments of joy saved us.

There are so many small incidents, small, random occurrences, chance meetings, kindnesses, that helped define me, that shaped me, that saved me. I've become small minded. I realize that phrase has always had negative connotations, narrow, shallow, stubborn. But I like it. I like being small minded, looking for the good in the smallest of places.

I'm done trying to be a big shot. My new goal is to become a small shot. I love small. I am so pleased I was the family runt. Because I was always so far down, I think it helped me to look up, embrace the power of small ideas, small moments, and I celebrate my heritage, small but sufficient.

PENTIMENTO

I've been trying my hand at poetry recently. I've never dabbled in this arena much, never truly understanding iambic pentameter and other terminology that sounds too much like math equations. I've always assumed poetry was for intellectuals who think differently than me. By different, I mean pedantic gobbledygook.

When you write poetry, I think you're supposed to make it impossible to read, even more difficult to understand. On that count I've done really well. Most of my poetry is very hard to understand, probably because it's a bunch of hooey.

I do have some awareness of poetry, like, for instance, dirty limericks:

> There once was a hermit named Dave,
> Who lived with a corpse in a cave;
> Said he, I'll admit . . .

Hold it right there! This is a really filthy poem and, believe it or not, I first heard it from my mother who fell apart telling it to me.

I sometimes go looking for ideas for poems, and sometimes poems come looking for me. I'll get a word, or a phrase stuck in my head like an earworm, and the only way to get rid of it is to try some poetry, and see if I can come up with an interesting rhyme that I haven't heard before.

Very recently, after a vacation in Italy, I somehow came across the word pentimento. It's a beautiful word used in the world of artists and museum curators to describe a process of painting over something.

It is also a word you hear all the time if you are a religious person. The root word gives us penitent, a person who is working hard to get away from the clutches of sin. By doing good deeds or helping to clean up the mess he or she has created, that person is doing penance. These two things make up the act of repentance—setting things straight and making a commitment to change and improve. These words all come from the Latin word pentimento.

What both of these disciplines, art and religion, have in common is the overall desire of an individual to get things right. Make changes for the better, painting over, starting over, improving every day. Great concept. But very hard to write a poem about. I tried and tried, but couldn't do it.

Back to painting, or repainting, for a minute. Apparently, even brilliant artists sometimes change their work.

Let's say a famous painter, like Leonardo DaVinci, started a painting of, let's say the Mona Lisa, and after a first attempt he doesn't like Lisa's smile. (Or is her name Mona?) He grabs some paint and covers over the original smile and shouts out, "That's the ticket," or in Italian, "Questo è il biglietto." Many artists painted and repainted their works.

Years later, scientists have discovered that they can use x-ray machines, or infrared reflectography, to look below the top layer of paint and see what's underneath, evidence that even the geniuses of the art world were frequently unhappy with their work.

I thought my poem could be, symbolically, about the experiences and trials in life that, layer-by-layer, paint a picture of who we are and, possibly, what we wish we had become, using paint the color of which is "regret." Hundreds of years from now your descendants may want to take your personal painting to an art historian for clues about who you were, never knowing the real you because you covered up the lessons you learned from your journey.

Bring in an x-ray or an infrared spectrometer and let's have a look underneath. It will reveal the real story of you, or, possibly, conceal all evidence of your flaws, or that you were not the character you pretended to be. Conversely, if you painted with the brush of humility, the colors of conscience, the warm sepia tones of honesty and courage, there may be discoveries of a very different sort.

The new technology has revealed that many of the masters would make a preliminary sketch, or under painting, then go back and add to it. Other artists preferred the honesty of going from blank canvas to finished product while feeling the painting, letting the emotion of a scene do all the work.

A poem about this would be a nice way to describe those who fill their lives with spontaneous moments of unplanned madness, energetically slapping up paint with abandon. Others prefer the carefully planned approach, sketches first, careful mapping, hesitant to ever stray off carefully marked pathways.

The random approach may come with a few regrets. The strict, planned approach, conversely, may disappoint you in the end. Your reaction to either of these scenarios may be to re-use the canvas because the first attempt was a disaster. You may be disappointed in parts of your personal tableau that needs some small correction. Or a lot. Cover over it, *pentimento*.

It is curious, to me, that the word "repent" and "repaint" are almost exactly the same word—talk about a cool literary device. So I tried to write a poem about this very bouncy word, *pentimento*. But I just couldn't find enough meaningful rhymes to pull it off.

Here's just a partial list of rhymes that came to mind. None of this was very useful in crafting a lovely sonnet.

Red Pimento: a red thing of dubious origins and even dubious-er flavor stuffed into a green olive in an attempt to make the olive taste better. They also tried putting them in cheese and bologna, a disastrous idea.

Cheap Memento: an object you picked up on a trip and then five years later forgot why you bought it and chuck it in the trash.

Sentimental: This is a condition brought on by throwing away the memento mentioned above and thinking, "Gosh, I wish I had kept that."

Transcontinental: They built a railroad across the country and connected it in Utah, when Utah wasn't cool. ("What, Utah still isn't cool?")

Spare Mentos (Breath Mint): These are so good that no one ever has a spare, and won't share with you if they did, so don't ask.

No More Bento: Bento is a box of yesterday's sushi, some dry, over-cooked salmon, and even before you leave the restaurant you'll think, "What a mistake. No more Bento."

Occidental: This is an adjective describing Western nations. Doesn't really rhyme anyway.

Accidental: Hmm. It's a poem about mistakes and covering them up. Might be something there.

Lament, Oooooh: Maybe you're sad about a bad decision and you cry out in pain and sorrow.

Presidential: It doesn't really rhyme (sort of) but it has the right number of syllables, and it's a quality we haven't seen in a very, very long time.

I'm sure he meant to: As in, "He was a nice guy but I'm sure he won't call me again."

Made a Dent. Oh, Oh: Frequently uttered by my wife who regularly crunches front and rear fenders on our cars, like she recently did in our brand new, one week old, luxury sedan.

Who Do You Know: In the era of social media it's about seeing and being seen. You don't ever want to walk into a party alone unless you've cleared it with your Facebook posse.

A-Rod and J-lo: The latest couple of choice of the paparazzi. We watched their lives under a microscope, shocked with their break up. Gee, I didn't see that coming.

Crescendo: Getting louder and louder and louder, kind of like presidential politicking as we get close to the November election. Another word for noise pollution.

A Very Long Concerto: I have sat through (or snoozed through) a number of orchestral performances. I like them, but you must agree that some composers went on way too long.

I Don't Think So: Something a dad says constantly to his 17-year-old daughter who wants to wear very, very short shorts out in public.

No, No, No: This is what you tell a dog that just peed on your rug. It's also something you might say to me; No, no, no, please don't write a poem about pentimento.

You see, not much there. It was an interesting attempt, and I had some fun with it. I also had some illumination about my personal journey, where I've been, what I've done with my life. There are certain things I would absolutely choose to *not* do again, mistakes I'd *love* to paint over. But for the most part, I've loved living on my terms; living at my pace; hitting or missing goals and aspirations. I've loved randomly slapping some paint on canvas just to see what happens. I love being arbitrary and spontaneous. I appreciate my missteps and have learned painful lessons from wrong choices. I've learned that the secret of great art is understanding contrast. Light and shadows. Illumination and darkness.

There isn't a single masterpiece anywhere in my personal art gallery. No one is auctioning off my work to the highest bidder, nor examining it with fancy technology to prove that it's authentic. Or a fake. But painting the story of my life, mixing colors and textures, capturing light, creating dimension and contrast, has been a creative explosion of enlightenment and introspection. When I stand back a few steps and see the whole thing, from a bit of a distance, you know what? I like it. I'm not going to change a thing.

> *I hereby swear*
> *to never write a poem*
> *about the concept of "pentimento."*
> *It's much too difficult and,*
> *in the end,*
> *I never meant to.*

FOLDING LESSON

I take naps every day. Retirement allows me this luxury. My age and my health demand it.

The couch in the living room is adjacent to the fireplace. In winter it's nice to nap in that room. There is a throw hanging over the arm of the sofa, perfect for afternoon siestas. "Throw," if you haven't heard, is the new name for blanket. We have throws, thrown on nearly everything in the house. They are different textures, different colors and styles, different fabrics. They must match the décor of the room in which they hang.

Throws are very popular, on and off a bed. You may take one to the park or to a football game. You can get a throw emblazoned with a large, family photo. You can get one with the colors of your favorite sports team. I saw a throw recently with a large photo of a can of Budweiser beer. These new, cuddly, cozy, caregivers are frequently given, happily received as gifts. It seems you can never have enough throws.

I stood up from a recent nap and, following strict instructions from my wife, carefully folded the throw and placed it at the foot of the bed where I found it. Never, never leave one of these treasures in a heap on the floor. Fold it. Replace it.

I am now going to make a sexist, misogynistic, narrow-minded, statement about women. Women were born to fold. It is in their DNA. Folding is as natural as nesting, nurturing, nursing. They can't help themselves. It is as natural as cooking and cleaning and changing diapers. (Settle down ladies, just having fun.)

Men can't fold. I've tried. My mother, all five foot two of her, could pull a king-sized sheet, fitted with elastic corners, out of the drier, give it a shake, flip and flop and push one corner diagonally to the other side, folded into a perfectly flat square, stacked it in the linen closet faster than any man can find the "on" button to the drier. Her sheet never touched the ground. If I fold a fitted king sheet it looks like a formless, shapeless, Egyptian-cotton blob.

When I fold a sheet, it is crooked. When I fold a towel, it is crooked. I can't even fold a washcloth and keep it straight. I can't hang a pair of pants on a hanger without getting wrinkles in them. Folding socks is anathema to me.

Recently, after my nap, I held the light-weight green throw in the air, pulled left corner over to right corner, shook it to let wrinkles settle, folded it in half again, vertically, shook it, then set it artfully at the foot of the bed where it resides full-time. (It's actually not green, more of a gray-mountain sage color, a palette approved for that room only.)

Moments later, Jill walks by the room. "Mark," she commands, in a voice that sounds like a summons to a folding clinic. I walk back down the hall, head lowered, eyes down, slinking like our schnauzer with muddy feet who knows he's in trouble. "How hard can it possibly be to fold that throw straight?" she asks. I think this is known as a rhetorical question, if I'm not mistaken. The actual definition of rhetorical is "don't answer."

"It looks straight to me," I say, feebly.

"Watch." She conducts a flawless seminar on the art of folding.

"Why does it have to be folded. It's called a throw? Why can't I just throw it."

"Don't be cute with me mister," she cautions as she turns and walks down the hall, the gray-mountain-sage throw a perfect geometric hexahedron, crisp lines as if it had been run over by a steamroller on hot asphalt.

Folding is a curious word with a variety of uses. For instance, you can fold if you have a bad poker hand. A sports team may fold under pressure. Lambs may be brought to the fold. Your business may have folded during the Covid Quarantine. Cartographers and geologists may call an undulation in the land, a "fold."

There is a variation on this word, "enfold." At its root this word is a synonym for 'embrace'. To enfold someone is to take them in your arms, squeeze tight, hold on, let them feel your strength. Let energy pass from you to them. Transfer love. Nothing quite like a warm hug. It doesn't matter how big or small your arms, or how tight you squeeze. The only thing that matters is doing it. It's the act of embracing that does the trick.

I'm still practicing the art of folding. It may take a lifetime to perfect. I'm not ready to take on king-size fitted sheets just yet. That is a fold too far. You may be fold-challenged like me, but you can master the art of enfolding. Tonight, take someone in your arms and enfold them. Envelop them. Embrace them. Wrap them up as tightly as you can. Unlike the art of folding a blanket, the art of enfolding doesn't have to be perfect. Even a clumsy attempt is good enough.

UNO

The game of *Uno* is a card game for kids. At least that's who I've played it with. It's simple to learn and its fun for adults and kids to play together.

This is not a complex game like *Call of Duty.* This, and other games like it, are violent games, played online, that involve shooting and killing as many people as you can. It is a popular game for men 35-plus years old, bored, athletically challenged, societal misfits with addictive personalities who have failed to grow up, and who stay up all night playing with others of their bug-eyed friends around the world in massive violent mayhem.

Uno is a very simple game of cards, the goal of which is to get rid of all your cards and dump them on another player. It is not played on-line with strangers. There are no guns or grenades in a dystopian world. It generally involves a few folks around the kitchen table.

In the digital world of virtual reality and three-dimensional, immersive entertainment, *Uno* doesn't have much appeal to the new generation living in augmented reality. These new technological wonders require skill, practice, timing, hand-eye coordination, and time. Lots of time. You don't simply set foot in these new three-dimensional environments and immediately start slaying dragons, or driving your space craft at warp speed, dropping bombs, or chopping off heads. It's hard. And one other thing, it is so realistic that it may cause motion sickness.

I've never experienced vertigo, or acrophobia, or nausea while playing *Uno*. You pretty much just sit there and draw cards from a deck, taking whatever card comes along. No skill is required. No hand-eye coordination. No quick reflexes. No one trying to shoot you.

The only real excitement in *Uno* is when you reach for the deck and come up with a reverse card. I'm not going to explain the whole game, you'll have to buy one and give it a go. Said simply, the reverse card lets you change the direction of the action, which is pretty much going around in a circle, sloughing cards from your hand. With this reverse card, you penalize other players, help yourself, and speed up your chances to empty your hand.

That reverse card, the one that gives you the power to change the flow of the game, is an interesting notion. A random draw of a card empowers you to change directions.

In heavy traffic one afternoon, cars backed up several city blocks at a complete stand-still, I missed a chance to do a good deed. It became an *Uno* moment. It was a very small chance to help someone in need, and after the fact I found myself wishing I had a reverse card, a do-over card, a second-chance card.

The cause of the traffic mess was an elderly woman, car stalled, right in the middle of one of the busiest intersections in our town. Yes, we have congestion problems even in our small city. She was clearly frustrated, afraid to step out onto the street. She had no phone, no idea about why the car died, or how to get it going again. The light turned red, and I stopped my car right next to hers on the left. I rolled down my window, "Is the car completely dead? Could you be out of gas? Is the battery dead?" Then this, "Stay in your car, I'm going to pull over and give you a push out of the intersection."

"What?" she said. "I can't hear you. What should I do?" she pleaded.

"Stay in your car, I'll . . . BEEEEEEP. BEEEEEEP. Horns started howling, cars started moving like leaf cutter ants with a piece of leaf on their backs, helter-skelter, direction-less, making everything more chaotic.

Jill had her hand on the door, ready to spring into action. "Don't get out of the car in this traffic, you'll get run over," I barked.

She said, "We've got to help her."

"Yes, yes, I can see needs help. What are you going to do? You know nothing about cars. Just stay in the car. Let me pull over. We need to push her car out of the intersection."

With that, I began looking for a way to pull my car off to the side of the road so I could help push the stalled vehicle. The traffic was backed up, all four lanes plus the turn lane, frozen, gridlocked. When the light turned green, cars began going around the poor woman on the right, honking horns, further frustrating her, leaving me with no chance to get to the curb.

Someone must help her. Someone must act. Someone has got to do something. I can't get over to the curb. Horns blaring, tempers flaring in the one-hundred-degree weather. Someone, somebody, some . . .

It would have to be some other Samaritan. Someone else would have to help. It wouldn't be me. There was no way for me to stop and lend a hand. Nothing I could do. It was too dangerous. If I had stopped my car, I would have made the log-jam worse. If I had helped the elderly woman out of the car, I may have put her, and myself in danger.

The pros, the cons, the rights, the wrongs, the choices, the options for helping this unfortunate driver, all passed through my head in seconds, the firing of a synapse. The surge of cars pushed me along, a tidal wave, a tsunami of cranky commuters cornered me and made it impossible to stop and help.

At least that's how I remember it. What if I had tried just a bit harder? What if I had just jumped out of the car and acted? Would some additional strong, younger men have joined me in pushing the stalled vehicle to safety? I'd like to think so.

There is no end to the story. We didn't stop. I'm still confident that there was, indeed, very little I could do. I have no idea how it turned out. It was not a giant catastrophe, no one was in any serious peril, and it, likely, took just a few minutes to sort out a routine situation.

But I did miss an opportunity, however small it now appears. I haven't been moping about, awash in a sea of regret, condemning myself for my cowardice or my inaction. It was a fleeting moment.

But I have, of late, been thinking, in a much broader sense, about missed opportunities that may, from time to time, come our way. Chances we didn't take. A helping hand we didn't offer, a helping hand we refused. An apology that didn't get offered, a rebuke, a reprimand, a scold, a harsh word blurted out in anger and haste. A decision that made you look good but made someone else look bad. Jumping to conclusions, impatience, quick to judge, slow to forgive. A job you didn't take, a girl you didn't kiss, a heart left un-mended, a promise broken.

Hand me an *Uno* reverse card and let me reverse and undo mistakes, right wrongs, try again, try harder.

This is something they do when filming a movie. Another take. Another chance for the actors to get their lines right. Another chance to create more drama, more tension, more emotion. Keep shooting until you get the scene right.

The game of real-life ought to have a reverse card, a change of directions. A do-over. A rewind button. Another take. A second chance. A re-write of your storybook, edited and improved.

Those of us who are not bilingual may mistakenly read the word *Uno* as, "you know." It takes practice to know, or recognize those singular opportunities to help or offer someone a hand. It takes practice to recognize "*Uno* moments," fleeting opportunities to gather yourself and make good decisions that are singular in nature. And if you don't get it right the first time, keep tossing cards. Somewhere in the deck is the highly coveted reverse card, a second chance to do the right thing. It's a very simple game to learn.

THE STALE FORTUNE COOKIE

During the time we have been behind prison walls, in solitary confinement, a total lock down due to the corona virus, I've been looking for things to do to keep from going crazy. I thought about making a shiv but didn't want to grind down one of our good spoons. I've tried planning a daring escape, but there isn't a single inch of razor wire, no moat to swim, not a single guard tower to circumnavigate. I tried banging my tin cup on the metal bars to protest the living conditions, but my wife just hollered, "Stop banging that stupid cup on the table."

"It isn't the table, it's the bars on my cell," I answered.

"Stop banging that cup or I'll show you a jail cell, mister." I'm not sure what that meant. I stopped banging.

With this new-fangled social distancing thing I decided to clean up my desk and reorganize a bit. I created some new files to get hard copies of some documents off my desk; reorganized my computer desktop; deep cleaned and disinfected the whole room. Then I started cleaning out the drawers, throwing out a bunch of stuff that would provide the courts with credible evidence of hoarding. Weird, useless, little things just have a way of sticking around.

I found a fortune cookie. It could have been from last week or it could be 2-3 years old. Of course I thought about eating it. How bad could it be? They're so crunchy; even if they're fresh they still feel like they could be stale. They are the most unsatisfying, tasteless, bland little confection but we always wish the restaurants would give us a couple more.

I cracked it open and pulled out the little slip of paper inside and read it.

"Make Happiness Happen."

From my self-imposed exile to the Isle of Patmos, spending so much time finding ways to fill the time, turning to tedium and triviality, caught up in excruciating boredom, the little adage rang a bell. This is not earth-shattering news. You've heard this before. It's not exactly Freudian, or Wertheimer's Gestalt, or even the ridiculous sugar pop-psychology from the Mickey Mouse Oprahian or Dr. Philian schools of thought. But it called out to me in a way that might otherwise have been a throwaway.

"Make Happiness Happen." Is there a formula? Is there a YouTube Video? Is there a recipe like making cookies? Is there a way to whip up a batch of happiness and make it happen?

It's a command: Make it Happen.

Jimmy Durante (if you're under the age of 60, you'll have no idea who this is) popularized an old song: "Make someone happy. Make just one someone happy. And you'll be happy to."

It called to mind an article I saw some time ago, something I saved but couldn't find because I just reorganized my desk, my files, and my digital desktop. It took several days of searching through my newly reorganized office but did, eventually, find it. It is written by Emily Fletcher for *The Huffington Post*, a digital news site.

It goes into some detail about our brain and something called neural pathways. She talks about some research that demonstrates that there are ways to activate these pathways and increase production of dopamine and serotonin, which travel pathways to the bliss center of the brain.

Emily compares this to a walk in the woods. When you start out, there may not be a pathway to follow, but over time a path gets worn from repeated use and the pathway becomes clearer, easier to follow.

"Our brains work the same way," she points out. "The more times a neural pathway is activated (neurons firing together), the less effort it takes to stimulate the pathway the next time (neurons wiring together)."

"Because of this, what we put our attention on grows," she writes. "If we're constantly looking at the negative and searching for problems, the neural pathways for negative thinking become stronger. But practicing gratitude can shift our attention to look for what is going right instead of looking for problems to solve. Over time, this encourages our brains to more consistently search for the constructive themes in our life instead of the destructive ones, helping us water the flowers instead of watering the weeds."

This author seems to have uncovered compelling research from psychiatrists, neurologists, and other experts who all agree that it's possible to carve these neural pathways in our brains.

How? I have two suggestions: 1-Practice gratitude. 2-Make happiness happen.

Start blazing some trails through the jungle of doubt, the forest of anger and resentment, the deep, dark woods filled with anger, jealousy, self-pity and, like a coyote off in the distance, howling the haunting refrain, "why me." You can, literally, carve the trails, firmly etch neuron pathways in your brain, and regularly improve your brain's pleasure center.

Practice gratitude. Practice and do the things that make you grateful to be alive, grateful to be healthy in a frightening world, living, sharing, and comforting others around you. We can learn, with practice, to be more thankful, to practice being more charitable, and show greater love for others.

"Gratitude can be a natural antidepressant," this author explains. "Practicing gratitude, therefore, can be a way to naturally create the same effects of medications and create feelings of contentment. Gratitude is like going to the mental gym; strength training for your neural pathways, if you will. The more you practice feeling grateful, the stronger that muscle gets. And over time, the workouts that at first seemed so challenging become easier and easier to do."

They've started printing your "lucky" lottery number on the back of the little papers inside the fortune cookies, and I suppose many people take that number to the nearest lottery store and buy a big stack of cards. Lotteries are still random and depend on luck, of course, and I doubt anyone has ever won the big jackpot by heeding the advice of a fortune cookie. But I do think it's possible to hit a jackpot of another kind.

"Make Happiness Happen."

We have a friend that we refer to as our 4th daughter. As a teenager, Riikka came from Helsinki, Finland to live with us for a time. She is still very much part of our family. Eventually, she married and moved away and we've kept in touch with her ever since. Nearly twenty years ago her husband was killed while deployed in Iraq. She was left with four children to raise, and it has been extremely difficult. She has really struggled.

It seems to me that her neural pathways, her trails through the woods, were destroyed and covered over by weeds and leaves and other detritus. It has taken years for her to blaze new trails, to practice gratitude, and to make happiness happen. But she's getting there.

She had a birthday recently and on social media posted beautiful pictures of flowers and one spectacular sunset with her caption, "Grateful tonight for God's gorgeous creations." She's finding beauty again because she's looking for beauty again. I believe she's finding joy again because she can find joy in even the smallest things. She seems to be finding happiness again because she is taking walks and beating trails in the woods, trails that lead to her brain's pleasure center.

I'm so happy to see her happy again, grateful for her gratefulness. I celebrate her joy. Riikka gave me permission to tell this story and she thanked me for helping her to see how far she has come.

Here's to blazing new trails, new adventures along your important, new neural pathways of gratitude. While quarantined and hiding against Covid19, or the myriad viruses and plagues and challenges and meltdowns yet ahead, no one is preventing you from taking a hike in the woods of gratefulness. Start hiking.

SORROW PREPARES YOU FOR JOY.

IT VIOLENTLY SWEEPS EVERYTHING

OUT OF YOUR HOUSE,

SO THAT NEW JOY

CAN FIND SPACE TO ENTER.

ORTHOGRAPHIC NEIGHBORS

I love words, word origins, word meanings. I'm trying to be a better writer and that means finding new words, underused words, unexpected words and phrases, so that I have, at the ready, the very best words I need to help tell a compelling story.

During my career in advertising and marketing I was frequently retained as a brand strategy consultant. On many occasions this included creating a name and identity for my clients. I frequently searched word origin sites to find words that may be used as a new company's name and web site.

We are living in an era when the drug manufacturers of the world are continually launching new drugs to make us healthier. You can't watch TV without hearing about four or five new medicines with the strangest sounding names. Ambian, Ajovy, Dupixent, Elliquis, Humira, Myrbetriq, Soliqua, Symbicort, Viagra. In medicine alone, our language is gaining dozens of new words, proper names, and pronouns at the least. We are also learning about side effects we've never known about, but that's a story for another day. (Do I really want to take a pill that causes anal leakage or, far worse, suicidal thoughts?)

The quarantine we have all endured left me with lots of

free time. I spent a lot of time at the computer, writing and, to use a modern business term, "ideating." Along the way, I stumbled onto a few words that intrigued me, words that are nearly identical but are very different with the change of a single letter. Hiss/Kiss. Care/Cave. Hear/Near. There are dozens of these words, same length, one letter change. There is an actual name for this called "Orthographic Neighbors." You may want to play a game with your kids to see how many of these words you can come up with. (No cheating allowed by looking them up on Google.)

There are other words, probably hundreds, that completely change meaning simply by adding or subtracting a letter, changing the length of the word along with changing its meaning.

Just for fun I started making a list, a random, pointless list, but curious to me. I noted how a simple tweak can completely alter the meaning of the word.

Here are a few I came up with along with a note about how a single letter change made the words completely opposite one another.

- **Cave/Care**

You may choose to live away from people, alone, withdrawn, well hidden in a dark place, or make a choice to serve others and learn the power of caring, the joy of service to fellow man.

- **Hiss/Kiss**

What a snake does to express anger; what a lover does to express love.

- **Repent/Repeat**

Change, improve, move on, resolve to do better, or continue to make the same mistakes again and again.

- **Repent/ Repaint**

True change for the better, or slap on some paint to simply cover mistakes or to hide flaws.

- **Holey/Holy**

Holey means having holes, as in modern jeans, ripped or torn; Holy is mending holes, fixing what is broken, looking to heaven for help so you can live life more wholly.

- **Exist/Exit**

There may be days when you feel like you are barely living, bored, just getting by. Time to take the first exit, a place you've never been. Go exploring, get lost.

- **Decent/Descent**

He was such a good man, so decent and respected, then he turned to bad things and went downhill, a steep descent.

- **Blight/Bright**

You can look at life as a dark, meaningless place, or a world full of light, hope and opportunity. You may think our country is in trouble, divided, or you can see America, as the land of opportunity, still, very much, a light on a hill.

- **Freeze/Free**

We get frozen, habitual, stuck in ruts, addicted, frozen in place, unable to move. But we can find personal freedom, recognize our freedom to move, change, elevate, explore unlimited opportunities.

- **Fact/Facet**

Truth verses slices of the truth; honesty and integrity verses trying to look shiny, scintillating. (Everyone loves a clown, that's a fact. But you may want to consider every facet of the job if you are thinking of becoming one.)

- **Marsh/March**

You can get stuck in the mud, unable to go on, or boldly move forward.

- **Rush/Hush**

No matter your age or circumstance, we all are in a rush. Don't deny it. Life is a rush, and it's wearing us out.

Slow down, find a retreat, a quiet zone, and go from rush to hush.

- **Crate/Create**

You may feel restricted, boxed in, living within a confined space, bored. But you can break walls and make the world exciting through innovation and invention, new ideas, creative adventures.

- **Hearing/Healing**

People tell you how to be strong, how to move on, how to grow and improve. Listen to the advice of others who love you, and let the healing begin.

- **Despair/Repair**

Life may be gloomy, sad, filled with sorrow and regret. But you can change, get better, fix your broken heart.

- **Alter/Altar**

You may hear something from the pulpit or the place where you worship that completely changes your life.

- **Down/Dawn**

I love this. When you feel low, down in the dumps, morning is coming with the sunrise.

- **Mourning/Morning**

See above.

- **Abused/ Amused**

People are lying to you, insulting you, harassing you, bullying you. You can choose to let it drag you down, let others define you, or you can choose to spend time looking for people who love you, entertain you, lift you, strengthen you, make you laugh and fill you with joy.

- **Rest/Rust**

This is an athletic term when talking about a team or a player with too much time off. Too much rest may make you rusty. Keep playing, keep working hard, stay in "game shape."

- ### Star/Start

You have a goal, a dream, an ambition, but it may seem out of reach, a distant star. You'll never know until you start, get going, stop dreaming.

- ### Old/Bold

You may be getting old, but it doesn't mean you have to sit around being old. Be bold, energetic, invent, create, act young and be young at heart. Live a full life of passion and pleasure and heed the advice of Dylan Thomas, "Do not go gently into that good night."

- ### Invert/Invent

Feeling upside down, troubled? Hanging over a cliff by your feet? Find your way right-side up with new approaches to life you've never tried.

- ### Hole/Hope

This may be my favorite. You may have dug yourself a hole, deep in trouble, isolated from family and friends, in the dark, alone, but know that there is always hope, there is always a neighbor who extends a hand and lifts you out.

- ### Meager/Eager

I may not be rich or famous. I may have little means, but I am anxious to live an abundant life filled with happy moments and passion.

- ### Ratings/Rantings

The news media gets one by doing the other.

- ### Soar/Sour

One simple letter turns "sour" (angry, bad attitude, resentful, as in "you old sourpuss) into soar. Rise above the pettiness and jealousy. Fly away.

- ### Forge/Forget

These words came to me as we recently remembered the 9/11 terrorist attacks. It was a time of fear and uncertainty, but we vowed to never forget the tragedy and the deceased and forged a new human bond, resolved to move on, determined to make a new start.

- ### Trial/Trail

Your journey may have been filled with trials, challenges, disappointments. Some may have been small. Others may have crushed you. Get off that road and blaze a new trail, a detour in your journey.

- ### Duet/Duel

This might be applied to your marriage. Are you singing together in harmony or is every conversation a duel? Find a new tune.

- ### Away/Aweigh

Some of us were taught to be good, but wandered away, strayed. No worries. (Aweigh is from the US Navy anthem "Anchors Aweigh," meaning anchors up.) We are on our way to a new destination, changing course, changing direction, knowing that help is up ahead in a safe harbor.

- ### Bright/Blight

Depending on the color of your glasses, the world is either a dismal mess, or it is filled with endless wonder.

- ### Sent/Scent

Though they sent you far away, your perfume lingers in the air.

- ### Desert/Dessert/Desert

This one is tricky because walking away from obligations means to desert; which may leave you wandering in the desert (a dry, desolate place.) But up ahead is a table filled with your favorite desserts, an oasis in the desert.

- ### Owe/Oww

I am indebted to so many people who fixed my brokenness.

I'll end with this one:

- **Chance/Change**

The recent pandemic has taught us all about resiliency and the need to adapt to change. We all had to change a bit, learn new ways to survive. Quarantines will do that. That's a Covid lesson. A nightmarish plague gave us a chance to change. Very simple adjustments to our lives have made a big difference. For better or for worse, everyone who survived the virus is forever changed.

I like this concept of "orthographic neighbors." A single letter changes everything. It makes me wonder if there are some very simple changes you or I could make in our lives. What small, basic flaws or imperfections do I have that could be fixed with a simple tweak? One simple addition or subtraction of change.

I am now on a quest to find more and more orthographic neighbors and other words with one or two simple letter changes. My list is growing longer and curiouser. And I'm hoping to find and embrace my human neighbors, friends, loved ones, who willingly, sometimes unwittingly, have made me feel better with simple acts of love, one simple act of kindness that touched me. One kind word that helped me get through the day. One small thing that changed my direction, changed my itinerary, set me on a new course, extended a hand, and pulled me out of the briar patch. One letter that changes a word; one small thing that changes your world from bad to good.

I'll **quit** now and be **quiet**. You get the idea. **Quite** clever, don't you think?

SUPER BLOOM

There were no blooms on my raspberry plants this year. Three rows of bushes and not a single bloom. This was the summer of extreme heat, and record-breaking drought, and the raspberry plants just couldn't get it going.

My blackberry bushes had more blossoms than any previous year, but in the heat, the berries were half their normal size and lacked the juicy, big-bang factor of these big, black beauties. There were more hornets/wasps/bees sucking the life out of the berries in larger numbers than normal, larger numbers than a biblical plague invoked by Moses on Pharaoh.

We drastically cut back on the amount of water we put on our lawns, and we ended up with some crusty, brown patches, weakening the turf and allowing weed growth. Nothing says drought quite like the invasion of morning glory vines, properly known as bind weed, which brazenly grows out of concrete and asphalt.

The hot summer is just a tiny part of my personal journey from hell. Here's an actual list of biblical plagues from my journal, documenting what I'll call the Covid years. Your list is likely as bad as mine. Or worse.

- Covid. I self-quarantined, kept away from everything, always wore a mask in public and got the virus anyway.
- Shingles. Nasty stuff broke out on my face, right

around my eye, threatening me with blindness
- Torn meniscus, knee surgery
- Diagnosed with Parkinson's Disease
- And, the largest invasion of grasshoppers in recent memory, descended on our valley

Autumn is coming but there will be very little color in the fall leaves. Heat and drought will do that. We expect the hillsides to be covered in a monochromatic wash of browns. The boredom and misery continue.

The Covid virus mutated and is coming back stronger than the first round. Experts have hinted that it may be around for a very long time. Anti-vaxers are on the march.

I'm not alone. Everyone has suffered hardships and challenges. My personal plagues are no different than yours, or those of the entire human race.

Elsewhere, The Anza-Borrego Desert State Park, the largest in California, had a super bloom this spring. We're happy to hear about this. California has had horrific droughts for many years and much of the state has been burning this summer, a result of dry, brittle trees everywhere. All the California smoke descended on our valley, adding gray skies, scratchy throats and burning eyes to our misery index. What's next? Turning our water to blood? Wait, we don't have any water.

According to *National Geographic,* a super bloom "is a colloquial term used to define an explosion of wildflowers that exceeds typical spring blooms." This phenomenon likely occurred because of So Cal's unusually rainy fall and winter, followed by cold temperatures, which "locked more moisture into the ground." Southeastern California deserts are covered in greenery, poppies, primroses, and lilies, according to a House Beautiful article.

This "explosion of wildflowers" in California deserts is so intense, BBC reports, that it can be seen from outer space.

As I sit in my den and look out at my brown lawn, brown hills, brown bushes, brown trees, tinder-dry flora everywhere just waiting for a rogue lightning strike, I am happy for Californians. Envious, but happy. It's a state still ablaze this summer of 2021, their tragedy quotient abnormally high. Yet there was this spring bloom. A rare, defiant super bloom. In one part of the state there was a bright spot, an explosion of color that attracted record numbers of painted lady butterflies from Mexico, laying eggs and helping to restore balance to the desert ecosystem.

What we wouldn't give for a super bloom; a global explosion of color; a pandemic of hope and optimism; a massive breakout of butterflies bringing a balm of balance and order. The California desert, awash in color, awash in renewal, reminds us that there are patches of light in dark places. There always have been. There are always individuals or entire communities that have it better than us, so many places worse off than us. There are people that live in abundance, others in desperation. It does no good to complain or compare. It does no good to be envious or bitter. But it is always good to dream of butterflies and flowers, lush green hillsides, lakes, and rivers flowing and filling with water, acres of deep brown earth and crops in fields. All these things are still there, here and there. They will all come again when the smoke has cleared, when the seasons change. The plagues will cease, the poets will write again, a page will turn.

A super bloom is coming. Expect it. It is not an entitlement, but it is the way of the planet, the way of earth, the way of heaven. Explosions of color after the darkness.

OARS IN THE WATER

Here's a small news article from CNN. I came across it on my digital subscription where I read 3 or 4 papers (or digital news sites) every day trying to keep up on current affairs. This article could have been easily missed or overlooked or viewed, by some, as non-newsworthy and uninteresting. It caught my attention, and I haven't been able to stop thinking about it. It's very short, barely a single paragraph, but very long on relevance.

Here's the entire story reported by CNN (On line, digital version):

Headline: "Three brothers from Scotland have set three world records after rowing 3,000 miles across the Atlantic Ocean in 35 days."

"Ewan, 27, Jamie, 26, and Lachlan MacLean, 21— known as BROAR, a combination of brother and oar—set out from LaGomera in the Canary Islands on December 12, 2019 and completed their 3,000-mile row to Antigua in the Caribbean on Thursday, PA Media news agency reported.

"Finishing the journey in Thirty five days, 9 hours and 9 minutes, the brothers have smashed several world records. The trio is the first three brothers to row any ocean, the fastest trio to row across the Atlantic, and the youngest trio to row across the Atlantic. (This is a good time to tell you how much I hate young people.) Atlantic

Campaigns confirmed the news on Facebook, adding that the siblings crossed the finish line playing the bagpipes.

"Previously, the record for a trio rowing the Atlantic Ocean was 41 days."

I'm not sure which element of the report surprised me the most. Rowing that far; their youth; their stamina; their determination; or keeping bagpipes in the boat. It sort of fits my unfair stereotyping that all Scots play the bagpipes. I'll keep, to myself, my opinions about men wearing skirts.

There was a photo, accompanying the story, of the boys, and their bagpipes. As you might expect, they were shirtless, their limbs bulging from their slender frames, tight and sinewy. No mention was made of what they ate for energy, how they kept hydrated, where they would sleep on the small rowboat, where they went to the bathroom, how did they keep their spirits up. Logical questions, really, that virtually all of us would think about.

The story didn't need mundane details as it turns out. A single paragraph spoke volumes. Their grit, their persistence, and their devotion to one another was story enough.

I'm comfortably into retirement now and would struggle to go 3,000 miles even in first class on a big airliner, or on a train or even in a luxurious automobile. I can't sit that long.

On a regular basis I worry about blisters, torn muscles, bad back, arthritis, and not getting too far away from a bathroom. No rowing for me. I like my comfortable surroundings and I have to have my adjustable bed where I sleep in the zero gravity position. I don't want to get on a boat of any size anymore, not a luxury cruise ship, not a speed boat, not a small dinghy or fishing boat, and certainly not a boat that requires me to paddle. Call me a crank.

But the three McLean brothers accomplished this seemingly impossible task with enthusiasm and commitment. They kept their eyes on the goal, even when it meant taking a shift in total darkness in the middle of the night, navigating by starlight.

My interpretation of the event is that the brothers didn't seem to focus on how hard it would be. They knew it would be hard. They signed on because it was hard. They focused not on the difficulty but on the challenge it would be, what a grand adventure it would be, what a grand victory over human frailties and human inclinations to doubt, groan, mumble, complain and believe it can't be done.

The BROAR got in the boat, set aside all doubts, and, for 35 days, pulled on the oars stroke by stroke by tedious stroke, night and day, hour after lonely hour. It seems a humanly impossible feat unless you have exceptional mental capacity and are loaded with the "patience" gene." It's a story of preparation, pluck, perseverance, patience, positive attitude, teamwork, and legendary Scottish fortitude to keep pulling on the oars, stroke by stroke by painful stroke.

I love the lesson of the BROARS and their incredible journey, setting a new record. 35-9-9. Somebody needs to put this on hats and shirts as a reminder that we can all do hard things.

The little folk song we all grew up with, generally sung as a round, comes to mind: "Row, row, row your boat, gently down the stream." It has a profound message: Get your oars in the water and start pulling. Pull together, focus on the end goal, work hard and life can be a dream. My stream, like yours, has a swift current, rocks that line the bed, white-water rapids, and it's a wild ride most days. The river will neither be crossed nor traversed without blisters, cramped muscles, hunger, discouragement and a powerful temptation to quit. It's long been called the "River of Doubt," and it's long and deep and treacherous.

But what an adventure. What a journey. What a ride. Your goals frequently fall by the wayside, right? Mine do. Keep paddling, pull, pull, pull. You don't need to get there in a hurry—it's a long journey, no records to break. Keep a steady hand on the rudder, your compass dry, and easy on she goes.

And listen for "Amazing Grace," off in the distance, blowing in the wind, played, on bag-pipes, long and low, by three very dedicated, very patient, very tired, Scotsmen waiting for you, just there, on the shore.

MORE BOOKS FROM MARK HURST

BIG SPRINGS

STILL THE RIVERS FLOWED

MILESTONES & MILLSTONES

PAIRFECTION

OUGHT 2

Made in the USA
Columbia, SC
27 July 2024

39401513R00076